MINISTER'S
HANDBOOK

A GUIDE TO REAL GOSPEL MINISTRY

MINISTER'S
HANDBOOK

A GUIDE TO REAL GOSPEL MINISTRY

CHAS & JONI STEVENSON

Stevenson ministries

Minister's Handbook
© Copyright 2023, 2015 by Chas and Joni Stevenson. All rights reserved.

No part of this publication may be reproduced, stored in a retrieval system, or transmitted in any way by any means, electronic, mechanical, photocopy, recording or otherwise without the prior permission of the author except as provided by USA copyright law.

Unless otherwise noted, Scripture quotations are taken from either the New King James Version / Thomas Nelson Publishers, 1982 (used by permission, all rights reserved), or from the King James Version, Cambridge, 1769 (used by permission, all rights reserved).

Published by:
STEVENSON MINISTRIES
5757 N Eldridge Pkwy, Houston, TX 77041
www.stevensonministries.org

Book design, cover design, interior design by Stevenson Ministries
Editors: Dawn Kopa, Delia Prince
Cover: Patrick McGraw

Published in the United States of America

ISBN: 978-0692416686

Table of Contents

Introduction 1

1. Discovering a Call 3
   - Ministry *Offices* vs. Other Ministries 4
   - Are You Called Into a Ministry Office? 5
   - Misperceptions About Being Called to a
     Ministry Office 7

2. Ministry Offices 13
   - Understanding Offices 13
   - Apostle 17
   - Prophet 22
   - Evangelist 28
   - Pastor 30
   - Teacher 33

3. Other Ministries and Gifts 37
   - Deacon 37
   - Helps 39
   - Governments (Administrations) 40
   - Life Gifts and Graces 41
   - Gifts of the Spirit (Manifestations) 43

4. A Minister's Responsibility 51
   - Our Scriptural Assignment 51
   - Understanding the Church at Large 55
   - The Care of People 62
   - Instant In Season and Out 64
   - Recognize the Need for All Offices 65
   - Expect Some Hardship 66

5. Ministry Preparation that Pleases God 69
   - Consecration 70
   - Commitment for a Lifetime 71
   - Passing the Tests 73
   - Mastering God's Word 75
   - The Holy Spirit—Your Best Friend 77

    Prayer and Fasting 78
    Apprenticeship 80
    Being Number Two, Three, or Four 81
    Full Speed 81
    Ministry Excellence 84
    Vision 87
    Sermon and Meeting Preparation 89
    Associations and Impartations 93
    Never Forget the Main Thing 95
    Beware of Major Pitfalls 97
    Ordination 99
    Missionaries 100

6. Money 103

7. Our 50+ Ministry Success Tips 111

8. Discipline and Conflict In the Church 135

    Resolving Conflicts 140

9. Sheep, Goats, Wolves, and Sheepdogs 143

    Sheep 143
    Goats 145
    Wolves 147
    Sheepdogs 150

10. Ministry Etiquette for Pastors and Traveling Ministers 151

    Etiquette for Pastors 151
    Etiquette for Traveling Ministers 155

11. Solid Doctrine 159

    Areas of Doctrinal Conflict 160

Other Theological Terms and Concepts 167
Suggested Resources 169
The Fellowship of the Unashamed 171
Bibliography 173
About the Authors 175

Introduction

In one sense, all Christians are called to serve God full time. Rather than endlessly wonder, *What am I called to do?*, we first have an obligation to Scripture. We are all called to minister *outside* the Church, and we are all called to minister *inside* the Church. For anyone searching for their ministry, here it is—He has "given us the ministry of reconciliation…and has committed to us the word of reconciliation" (2 Corinthians 5:18-19). God has already commissioned every single one of us to one universal gospel ministry of restoring people back to Him. Every single Christian has been told by Jesus to "Go into all the world and preach the gospel to everyone" and "make disciples of all nations". We are all called to heal the sick, cast out devils, and minister life to a dead world. Outside the Church, we call it *sharing our faith* or *being a witness*. Every believer is to do it. And that never changes.

Inside the Church, we can call it the ministry of "one-anothering", as we are to love one another, serve one another, submit to one another, instruct one another, encourage one another, help one another, forgive one another, and so forth. Every one of us is to do it (Hebrews 6:10). And that never changes.

We don't need a title, a fancy ministry name, or our own non-profit organization to minister the gifts and love we have to others. According to Romans 12, all believers have been given "gifts differing according to the grace that is given to us". And we all have been chosen for a unique position within the Body of Christ and given a specific grace to fulfill it.

So, though every committed believer already has a ministry and a general call, this handbook is more specifically for the Christian who senses a subsequent call to a *Ministry Office* of Apostle, Prophet, Evangelist, Pastor, or Teacher, or to a clear leadership role within the Body of Christ that involves guiding and instructing Church members. The Lord needs strong Ministers who have a right, Scriptural perspective on their assignment. The Lord needs Ministers to understand the Kingdom of God, teach the Word of God rightly, and demonstrate His power through the Holy Spirit. The Lord expects Ministers to be fully equipped so that they can fully equip others.

Chapter 1
Discovering a Call

One of our church leaders told me this funny story of an old farmer friend of his who was a fellow usher at a previous church years prior. The farmer said that one day he saw a vision from God in the sky that read, "P.C.". He just *knew* that those initials meant *Preach Christ*, so he planned on being a Preacher somehow someday. But as time went by and as he struggled within himself to make it happen, he eventually came to realize that his interpretation was wrong all along. God wasn't telling him to *Preach Christ*. He was telling him to *Plant Corn*. Misinterpreting God's will can bring frustrating and confusing seasons to a person's life, especially in the area of *calling*. So, rather than words in the sky, prophetic words from friends, or personal excitement and zeal for the Lord that people mistake for a call to Ministry, they need a more clear leading from the Lord. And they need some Bible instruction about it. Far too often, church members mistakenly feel called to the Ministry, "waiting their turn" for something that is never really going to happen because God hasn't called them to it.

Ministry *Offices* vs. Other Ministries

1. **Ministry Gifts are given by Jesus**: Apostle, Prophet, Evangelist, Pastor, Teacher. We will call these *Ministry Offices* for the sake of distinguishing an *Office* from other gifts (see Chapter 3).

    > [He] gave gifts unto men...and He gave some, apostles; and some, prophets; and some, evangelists; and some, pastors and teachers; for the perfecting of the saints, for the work of the ministry, for the edifying of the Body of Christ: till we all come in the unity of the faith, and of the knowledge of the Son of God, unto a perfect man, unto the measure of the stature of the fullness of Christ (Ephesians 4:8, 11-13).

2. **Terminology**— the five Ministry Offices are what we have termed "Ministers" or "Preachers" in this handbook. The terms 'Ministry Office', 'Ministry', and 'the Ministry' will be capitalized when referring to the Offices that Ministers are called to. When referring to gospel ministry, ministry gifts, or ministry (serving) in a general sense that all people find a place in (not one of the five Ministry Offices), the words will not be capitalized. Granted, there are many people who serve in a support role in formal Ministry, supporting Ministers. But since they do not serve in a Ministry Office, then we will refer to what they do as ministry (not capitalized).

3. **Not everyone is called to one of these Offices.**

4. **Teaching, preaching, and healing**—those who stand in one of these Offices follow the pattern of Jesus for gospel ministry, which involves "teaching, preaching, and healing". A certain leadership anointing will accompany the Office, as well as a clear and effective speaking gift (teaching or preaching) to edify the Church.

5. **Other ministries**—music, prayer, outreach, and scores of other Church ministries and functions are not in the same category as *Ministry Offices*. Though there are other ministry offices referenced in Scripture, for clarification, this book will use the term *Office* only for Ministers.

6. **Not all Offices must exist in a local church**—though all five of these Gifts are essential in the development of believers, not all five must be present in any one church at all times.

Are You Called Into a Ministry Office?

The Lord alone calls people into Ministry Offices and graces them accordingly. A true Ministry calling is not a *career* choice. And it's not something to be ambitious about. The Church doesn't function that way. The Lord is the decider of *who* is a *what*, "But now God has set the members, each one of them, in the Body just as He pleased" (1 Corinthians 12:18). So, how can you know if you're called to an Office?

1. **Approach the question with fear and trembling**, for it is a holy and serious undertaking, "My brethren, let not many of you become teachers, knowing that we shall receive a stricter judgment" (James 3:1). Preachers are judged twice—once as a Christian like everyone else, and then again as a Minister.

2. **Know God's will**. Learn how to hear His voice, and know the inner witness of the Spirit. Far too many have relied on random coincidences, voices of family or friends, or so called prophecies that shouldn't have been prophesied. Be sure that whatever you hear confirms the witness of the Spirit in your heart, for no one can *call themselves*.

   Be certain about it, for there will certainly come a future day when you are tempted to wonder if you made the right choice and really heard from God. What you knew to be true from God in the beginning must still ring clear and true in the middle, for it may be your only anchor of confidence for continuing until the end.

3. **What grace do you really have?** For Ministry, the grace must be "extra". What gift of God burns within you? What grace, what ability, what anointing of God has been bestowed upon you to stand in an Office? Notice what ability just flows in you without much effort. Detect it, test it, and then be honest about it—did it edify people? The last thing anyone wants is to step into a place of Ministry without the grace to do it.

4. **Test the gift again and again** to be certain it's up to the level necessary for a Ministry Office. And don't rely only on feedback from your spouse, your family, or friends who want to be nice. A Ministry Office

requires that your gift can edify a group of people and not just one or a few. "For if anyone thinks himself to be something, when he is nothing, he deceives himself. But let each one examine his own work, and then he will have rejoicing in himself alone, and not in another" (Galatians 6:3-4). You should find yourself operating very comfortably and effectively in it. A Ministry Gift is not someone who is a "good communicator" or who can "preach really loud and excitedly". The proof is when there is an anointed touch of God on it, and people are drawn into the Spirit during the teaching or preaching.

5. **Are you qualified?** Are you solid in life and in faith? Do you really care about people, or is there another motive? How submitted to the Word of God are you? Do you have an ability to lead people? Ask these questions and more.

6. **Submit yourself and your gift to your Pastor** (or a seasoned, mature, Spirit-filled Church leader who is not your peer) for confirmation and recognition of what you are sensing from God. Those who have no accountability to any one above them are usually renegades and out of order.

Misperceptions About Being Called to a Ministry Office

1. **Mistaking zeal for calling.** We all want to please God and "stand complete in all the will of God." We all put effort into learning of God, serving God, and committing to God. We love the things of God and

we enjoy great gospel ministry. We love people, we're excited about the Word of God, and we want to be a fiery hot Christian. But never confuse fire and zeal for a particular call. All believers should be *that*. It doesn't mean a person is called into one of the Ministry Offices.

2. **I have a great testimony.** How God has impacted one's life is great and important, but a Ministry Office is much more than that, and Ministers must have a lot more in them than a testimony. All believers should have some sort of testimony. Testify and bless people every chance you get, but a great testimony gives no evidence of calling.

3. **I want to do something I love and care about.** That's a mistake as well. In truth, the most important thing in your life should always be God and His Kingdom. So, naturally, you're going to like the gospel better than anything in the world. It doesn't mean you're called.

4. **Money—maybe Ministry is how God wants to prosper me.** Nope. That motivation for Ministry is never of God. And you'll usually be quite disappointed in the pay.

5. **Secret, personal glory or feeling important.** Be very careful about what *self* is really seeking. Everyone wants to feel special. But everyone actually already is. Jesus has made all believers special. And Ministers are not more special than anyone else. Jesus has already given us His glory (John 17), so don't ever seek it. Attention and honor seeking (to be seen, heard, or applauded) are disqualifiers for any type of Ministry. Prominence—those who want it should never be given it. Those who don't want it,

qualify for it. For those who are pining away to be in Ministry, it's usually best if they're not. They should shelve that soul-ish desire until God has compelled them by His Spirit.

6. **But God has shown me that I am destined for great things.** Any time you hear "how great your Ministry will be" or how "the world needs you", you should know that God never says it like that. In a call, there is nothing about *you*, except, "Are you ready to sacrifice?" Recall when God called Paul the Apostle. He didn't tell him any grand thing of worldwide, 2000 years of influencing the Church, penning more than half of the New Testament. Rather, God emphasized, "tell him how great things he must suffer for My name's sake" (Acts 9:16). The call is never about *us*, but always about the *gospel*. Anything else is enticement from the devil and leads to selfish ambition and then corruption, so steer clear.

7. **I'm not satisfied in my current vocation. I've had a hard time with little success, so I think I'll give Ministry a shot.** That doesn't work. If people aren't successful at their natural job, they won't be successful at their spiritual one. Remember Jesus saying that if He can't trust people with unrighteous "mammon", how could they be trusted with "true riches"? Be sure that you are excellent and satisfied in your current employment before stepping into Ministry, or you'll carry the unsuccessfulness right in with you.

8. **But it must be so nice to work in a Christian environment, in a nice peaceful place like a church or ministry.** Never did the Lord instruct believers to

find a way to escape the world and its sinners. Rather, He has placed us right in the middle of them so we can provide some light in their darkness. Relish your time among the heathen, for that is the high calling for every believer.

9. **The Ministry is the best job in the world.** No it's not. The best job in the world is the one that God has called *you* to and the one He has given *you* grace to accomplish. A Minister who goes on and on about how wonderful it is to be in their position is misleading the people. We can all love what we do and recognize the honor of it, but acting like it's special or better than other vocations is wrong.

10. **The Ministry would be a lot easier than what I'm doing now**—anyone can get up and give a couple of speeches every week, right? Wrong. That's a sign of clear disqualification. That's like saying that an NFL quarterback must sure have an easy job because he only works three hours on Sunday. Real Ministry involves a full work week, subsequent to the formal services. Being the leader of a church or ministry is like being a small business owner (longer hours and total responsibility for every single thing that happens). And Ministry involves people—lots of people. And people aren't all that easy.

11. **I come from a long line of Preachers; surely I'm called.** This is not how it works under New Testament order. In the Old Testament, priestly callings were passed down in the family (of Levi). But in the Church, only the Lord Jesus decides who the Preachers are. And a son or daughter may or may not have an anointing to stand in an Office. Though family members can be part of a ministry

and serve faithfully in operations or administration if they have the grace to do it, it doesn't mean they're called to a Ministry Office. It's a mistake for Preachers to force pulpit ministry on their children or spouse to be the family "heir", when really there is no gift to support it.

12. **Becoming a Minister will help solve some of my problems.** Ministry doesn't solve our problems. It intensifies them. Ministry always and only exposes and fuels any existing issues. If a marriage has strain now, it will have it double in the Ministry. If you have lack of faith for money now, you'll have it worse in the Ministry. If you have stress now, you'll have more in the Ministry. The Ministry, regardless of the area of service, is an extremely strenuous calling.

Recent Survey Statistics

- 50% of the Ministers starting out will not last 5 years.
- Only 1 out of every 10 Ministers will actually retire as a Minister in some form.
- 90% of Pastors said the Ministry was completely different than what they thought it would be like before they entered the Ministry.
- 33% felt burned out within their first five years of Ministry.
- 70% of Pastors constantly fight depression.
- 50% of Pastors feel discouraged and want to do something else (Lane; Sherman).

Chapter 2
Ministry Offices

Apostle
Prophet
Evangelist
Pastor
Teacher

Understanding Offices

1. **Spiritual gifts don't automatically mean *Office*.** Though a person may seem to have certain qualities and even evidence the spiritual gifts associated with an Office, it doesn't mean the person stands in that Office. Going on mission trips doesn't make one an Apostle. Giving prophecies does not make one a Prophet. Leading people to Jesus does not make one an Evangelist. Being able to teach the Bible does not make one a Teacher. And caring about people does not make one a Pastor.

2. **Anointing, timing, and calling**—the *Office* is equipped with an additional spiritual endowment

and anointing that others don't have. And even when there is a call, there is also the timing of the Lord and the proving out of the particular anointing for that call before stepping into the Office.

3. **A Minister must have a teaching or preaching gift** that brings consistent edification and equipping to the Body and that can clearly *carry* meetings.

4. **A title does not prove the Office.** The fruit of the person's ministry is the proof, "we know them by their fruits". So, knowing the call is important. Flourishing in the gifts associated with that call is important. And bearing consistent fruit is important. Being titled is not as important. Philip "the Evangelist" was never called that until long after he had done the works and proved his ministry (Acts 21:8).

5. **The call of a Minister is not what he or she *does*, but who he or she *is*.** There is no separation, as the gift is not given *to* the Minister. The gift *is* the Minister.

6. **There are different measures and levels of anointing within an Office.** For example, some Pastors are graced with an ability to lead thousands, others hundreds, and others less. Some Teachers can teach a small group, while others can teach a large convention. Some Evangelists can minister to thousands, while others can't. The honor and respect for the Office at any level should remain constant.

7. **Not all Ministry Gifts look and sound the same**, even when of the same Office.

8. **All Ministry Offices need the same fundamental Ministerial training.** The unique training for a

particular Office can come subsequently, but emphasis must be placed on the training basics for all Ministers.

9. **It is possible to stand in more than one Office**, whether at different seasons of ministry, or even within the same season. However, one Office will usually tend to be more prominent in the person than the other.

10. **Bishops and Elders (for terminology purposes)**—the word 'Bishop' is used several times throughout the New Testament. A 'Bishop' is not a separate Office, but rather a more *general term* used for one of the five Ministry Offices. The word 'bishop' is from a Greek word, 'episkope', which literally means *investigation, inspection, and oversight*. A Bishop is an overseer of people, and can refer to any of the five Ministry Offices. A Bishop is one whose oversight of people allows him entrance into their lives to know them, exhort them, rebuke them, instruct them, investigate, and correct when necessary. In modern day, the term 'Bishop' is commonly used for Pastors, and more particularly for Pastors who have more than one church under them. So, some will change their title from Pastor to Bishop when they are 'pastoring' two or more churches. Scripturally, however, we have no distinction for Bishops being something more than one of the clear five Offices, but rather a term used in a more general sense to describe them.

The word 'Elders' is also a Biblical, more general term referring to Ministers. In Scripture, both the five Ministry Offices and also Bishops are frequently used synonymously with the word 'Elders' (Titus 1:5-6). Sometimes local churches use the term *elders* to denote their leadership, and it's fine to do so since the word can refer to seniority or age. But those are not necessarily Ministers.

11. **Character and Lifestyle Qualifications for Ministers**—solid in the Word, solid in life and lifestyle, solid in character, full of the Spirit, and wise. More than any other factor, the most prominent differentiator for called ones is *wisdom*. Good Ministers have a special social skills grace from God, knowing how to understand people, deal with people, and solve people problems. Wisdom from above compiled the book of Proverbs, which gives proper perspective for life, character, and interaction with people. Without wisdom, the Minister will never be the trusted "tree" to which people can run for answers and protection. "But the wisdom that is from above is first pure, then peaceable, gentle, willing to yield, full of mercy and good fruits, without partiality and without hypocrisy" (James 3:17).

    1 Timothy 3:1-7 and Titus 1:5-9 give some qualifications for a Minister (bishop, elder):
    - Blameless
    - the husband of one wife (wife of one husband)
    - not self-willed, temperate, sober-minded, self-controlled
    - of good behavior, not given to wine
    - gentle, hospitable, not violent, not quick-tempered

- able to teach, not quarrelsome
- not greedy for money, not covetous
- one who rules his own house well
- not a novice, lest being puffed up with pride he fall into condemnation
- must have a good testimony in the public lest the devil snares him
- holy, just, a lover of what is good
- keeper of sound doctrine—holding fast the faithful Word

Apostle

Apostle—a Minister of the Word who is sent by God to pioneer churches, impart foundation and direction to churches, and who has clear signs and wonders accompanying.

1. **There are three categories of Apostles:** *the Apostles of the Lamb, foundational Apostles,* and *Apostles today* (aside from the Lord Jesus Himself, who is in a class all His own).

    The twelve Apostles of the Lamb—"And the wall of the city had twelve foundations, and in them the names of the twelve Apostles of the Lamb" (Revelation 21:14). To be an Apostle of the Lamb, one must have physically walked with and known Jesus during His ministry on earth (Acts 1:21-22). The twelve include Peter, Andrew, James, John, Philip, Bartholomew, Thomas, Matthew, James the son of Alphaeus, Lebbaeus, Simon, and Matthias (Matthias replaced Judas Iscariot in Acts 1:26).

Foundational Apostles—the Apostles that the household of God, the Church, was built upon, "having been built on the foundation of the apostles and prophets, Jesus Christ Himself being the chief cornerstone" (Ephesians 2:20). These Apostles are the ones in the Bible who were the pioneers of this gospel, some of which had the unique responsibility of providing New Testament Scripture, "...by revelation He made known to me the mystery...it has now been revealed by the Spirit to His holy Apostles and Prophets" (Ephesians 3:3,5). The twelve Apostles of the Lamb are included in this category as well, but there were more than just the twelve. There were at least eleven more:

- Paul (Romans 1:1)
- Barnabus (Acts 14:14)
- James the brother of Jesus (Galatians 1:19)
- Epaphroditus (Philippians 2:25 – Though many translations use the word "messenger", it's actually the Greek work "apostolos".)
- Timothy and Silvanus (1 Thessalonians 2:6, 1:1, 3:2)
- Andronicus and Junia (Romans 16:7)
- Apollos (1 Corinthians 4:6-9)
- Two unnamed Apostles (2 Corinthians 8:23 —again, the Greek word "apostolos" but is translated here as "messengers".)

Apostles today—Nowhere in Scripture does the Bible say that the Office of the Apostle has been done away with. So, though we can admit that the foundation of the Church has been built and there is no room for any more New Testament Scripture ('canon') or "revelation of the mystery" (Ephesians 3:4-5), Jesus still appoints people as Apostles, and there is still a need for them today.

2. **Definition of 'Apostle'**—*a sent one, a delegate*. It can also mean *pioneer*; so in the context of the gospel, an Apostle tends to be one who establishes new churches and who penetrates places that have no gospel.

3. **An Apostle may influence the Church at large** as one *sent out with a special message or ministry* (along a certain Scriptural line) to the Church—the message of faith and power, or the baptism of the Holy Spirit, or to spearhead revivals or Bible schools, etc.

4. **Maintaining the foundation**—an Apostle is one who helps churches understand and maintain solid doctrine, keeping the foundation of the household of faith secure. Paul said, "According to the grace of God which was given to me, as a wise master builder I have laid the foundation, and another builds on it. But let each one take heed how he builds on it" (1 Corinthians 3:10). It makes sense that if the early Apostles built the foundation, Apostles today would be useful as an example in reminding us of that gospel foundation.

5. **Qualifications and spiritual gifts**—the clearest qualification is in the evidence. What fruit has come from the person's ministry? And then, what grace is really on them? Paul said there were *signs* of an Apostle, "Truly the signs of an Apostle were

accomplished among you with all perseverance, in signs and wonders and mighty deeds" (2 Corinthians 12:12). In addition to a grace to teach and preach, and in addition to a grace that would cause people to love God, walk with Jesus, and follow Him faithfully, a true Apostle would also have signs, wonders, and miracles evidenced in his or her ministry.

6. **An Apostle is a die-hard gospel distributor**, persevering through any tribulation to the get the Kingdom into the hearts of men.

7. **An Apostle has the anointing to operate in more than one Office as needed.** Apostles can function as an Evangelist when venturing into a new land, as a Pastor when starting or helping a church, as a Prophet when discerning the needs of the people, and as a Teacher when explaining the Word.

What an Apostle is *Not*

1. **An Apostle is not one who is above every other Pastor or every other Minister.** Some have thought that because Apostles are listed first in 1 Corinthians 12:28, they must be above everyone else. But that's wrong. "God has set some in the church, first apostles..." That doesn't mean they are the highest authority. It means they were the first ones put into Office, as the only Ministry Gift that existed in the beginning was the Apostle. Apostles would only be the authority in a church or organization that they have influence in and willing submission from others in.

2. **An Apostle does not have spiritual authority over everyone else.** They don't "govern" the Church. Though their office may be a premier office while establishing a new work, it would only be premier where God has graced them—somewhat like a CEO of a company, who may have authority in their own company, but certainly not at every other company. And even a CEO's authority is not sweeping dominance, but rather a limited authority submitted to a board and also to the shareholders. So, though an Apostle may certainly be sent to a city, a region, or a nation to pioneer works, it doesn't mean they are "over" all churches in that city, nation, or region.

3. **An Apostle is not one who goes around to random churches, making corrections** and trying to gather ministers under them. Of course, some Ministers may look to an Apostle to glean from, partner with, or submit to, but it's not initiated by an Apostle. The only authority and influence that an Apostle would have would be with churches that he or she's started, preached in, or had mutual relationship with church leaders in. Or with those who've asked for help and ministry.

4. **Every church and ministry does not need an Apostle over them as "covering".** It's more a personal and willing submission to those over us in the Lord with the purpose of accountability and honor, rather than "spiritual covering" mandated by God. Everyone needs a Pastor, and everyone should recognize "fathers in the faith". Every Pastor should be personally submitted to other Ministers. And when possible, every Minister should have a Pastor or

Elder who is over them in the Lord. But the New Testament never says that there is an Apostle nor Prophet over every church. Any Minister could be a Minister to other Ministers and to apprentices, spiritual sons, or students in the faith.

Prophet

Prophet—a Minister of the Word as a proclaimer, with insight into the spiritual dimension and a particular, divinely focused message to the Church.

1. **Old Testament Prophets, foundation Prophets, New Testament Prophets today**—Prophets of the Old Testament were God's only anointed mouthpiece (kings and priests had a different role). Foundation Prophets were New Testament Prophets that the household of God, the Church, was built upon, whom God first revealed the mystery to, "having been built on the foundation of the Apostles and Prophets, Jesus Christ Himself being the chief cornerstone", "[the mystery] has now been revealed by the Spirit to His holy Apostles and Prophets" (Ephesians 2:20; 3:4-5). There are no more of either of these two types of Prophets. But there are certainly modern day New Testament Prophets who function like the early Church Prophets, just without the role of foundation building and initial revelation of the mystery.

2. **Teaching or preaching, and leadership**—a Prophet will always have a clear teaching or preaching gift as well as a proven leadership quality about them—

enough to consistently edify a church congregation. And this is where the separation is made. Many people can be used by God in words of knowledge, words of wisdom, or prophecy, or miracles. But only those with leader qualities and those with a true anointing to preach to a group can stand in the *Office*. Remember, even though "you may all prophesy", the scriptures continue on saying "the spirits of the prophets are subject to the prophets" (1 Corinthians 14:31-32), which means that "prophetic" gifts, words, and ministry does not make one a full Prophet. All the gifts can be "catchy" at different times, and someone may excel in certain gifts in their life. But it still doesn't mean the person stands in the Office of Prophet. A true Prophet is anchored to the Word (not just the Spirit) and prepares much in the Word.

3. **Prophets have an element of divinely inspired speaking** under the power of the Spirit by inspiration at the moment or with inspiration for a future moment for a person or group.

4. **Prophets tend to awaken and activate saints to the purposes of God**—plans, times and seasons, transitions, or visitations, bringing a "now" message as the mouthpiece of the Lord to confirm His plans.

5. **Spiritual gifts**—a Prophet will have certain manifestations of the Spirit in their ministry. First, the simple gift of prophecy (not predicting, but *encouraging* and *lifting up*, "But he who prophesies speaks edification and exhortation and comfort to men"—1 Corinthians 14:3). Then, they will also have some of the revelation gifts operating

consistently: word of wisdom, word of knowledge, or discerning of spirits.

6. **Spiritual thrust**—Prophets tend to edify a church with a unique divine *push* upward and breakout from status quo that seems to almost leave a residue of strength in their wake. Prophets will tend to see into and tap into things in the spiritual dimension that reveal the spiritual needs present and then impart things that can help people, help local churches, or help the Church at large.

7. **Prophets are sensitive spiritual instruments** with an active "antenna" that is open to the spiritual climate and to what God is saying or doing. Old Testament prophets were referred to as *seers* (perceiving things supernaturally), which is still true of Prophets today. Prophets will not know and perceive everything, but only some and in part. However, not everything a Prophet sees should be said out loud or in public. Some things known are in order to minister to people, but other things are just an alert to pray.

8. **Examples of Prophets**—Agabus (Acts 11:28, 21:10), and several others (Acts 13:1). Prophets will have different ranks in the Body, different measures of the anointing, and unique, individual styles.

What a Prophet is *Not*

1. **A Prophet is *not* someone who is hyper-spiritual**, who constantly gives prophesies to others, or who is always having spiritual visions and dreams. Jesus didn't do that, and yet He was the greatest Prophet of all. Prophets shouldn't put prophesying above

preaching the Word. Prophesying is only a small part of a Prophet's ministry. And if prophesy is forced and over-emphasized, it can cause people to despise, de-value, and forget prophesies. A good Prophet is balanced with the Word and not overly spiritual, recognizing the legitimacy of teaching and preaching solid gospel truth. It is emphasized even of Jesus, that He went about *teaching, preaching,* and *healing*—not *prophesying* (Matthew 4:23, 9:35). Also, John the Baptist was a Prophet who came with *only* a gospel message. Prophets must resist the Old Testament influence of using complicated and hard to interpret symbols, with very complex and lengthy words that no one can decipher and that are impossible to analyze for accuracy. Now that the mystery has been revealed and Light has come, the dark sayings and confusing prophecies have turned into visions and dreams with *clear* interpretation (i.e. Peter quickly knew exactly what the carpet vision meant, and Cornelius knew exactly where to find him.)

2. **A Prophet under the New Testament does not have the same status** as a Prophet under the Old Testament. In the Old Testament, Prophets were the only ones to communicate with and speak for God. They were God's leaders, preachers, and watchmen. But now, all believers and Preachers can communicate with God, we can all have great spiritual discernment, and we are all called to watch and pray. And all believers and Preachers can speak for God at times. No longer is the anointing of God's Spirit reserved for the prophet, priest, and king, but now He is available for everyone so that we

don't have to wait on Prophets to give us God's message. For this reason, these Old Testament attributes of Prophets are no longer valid, such as "Surely God does nothing unless He reveals His secret to His servants the prophets" (Amos 3:7). And also, "... believe His prophets and you shall prosper" (2 Chronicles 20:20). There is no New Testament confirmation of those doctrines, so they didn't *pass through* the cross. Prophets today are brought to the same level and status as the other four Ministry Offices.

3. **New Testament prophets do not preach like Old Testament ones** because 1) Prophets are given to the Church, not to the world, the nation, the city, or the region. And 2) the message is no longer heavy on threat against sin and sinners. Now, the message is the gospel, the good news of salvation through Christ—the sin *remedy*. If Jesus didn't come to condemn the world (John 3:17), it's certain that he didn't send anyone else to. Prophets are not here to rebuke and threaten the nation for its immorality. They're here to edify the Church, just like the other Ministers. God sends the gospel to nations to save people rather than threats from Prophets to punish people. We see no example of any Apostle or Prophet attacking the governments of their day. We only see gospel preaching and Church discipling. For example, Agabus saw the coming drought in Judea, but didn't go find national leaders to blame it on and curse. Rather, this helped the disciples send aide to the *brethren* in Judea (Acts 11:28-29).

4. **Prophets are not given as the "big correctors" of people and churches.** All Ministers may occasionally

correct people or church practices, as "All Scripture...is profitable for doctrine, for reproof, for correction, for instruction" (2 Timothy 3:16). Some have wrongly thought that Prophets had a special license to be stricter with people because of their blunt personalities, even to the point of honing their harsh and pointed approach, thinking it was honorable to remain "rough around the edges". God is not like that, and neither is the Spirit. Even in conviction, the Spirit is never harsh, but gently firm.

5. **Prophets are not put in Office to lead and guide believers' lives.** Rather, every believer has the Holy Spirit in him to lead and guide him in life. So, it is unscriptural to seek such guidance from Prophets. Prophets may certainly give words that confirm guidance or leading, but it's wrong for a Prophet to let people seek it from them. Point them to the Word and the Holy Spirit within. There are no more Moseses leading the people in and out, here and there.

6. **A New Testament Prophet does not have the same requirement as Old Testament Prophets**, where every prophecy was required to be 100% accurate or else be classified as a *false Prophet*. (Before the Holy Spirit lived inside all believers, this was the only way to reveal what was of God and what was not.) Most of the Old Testament prophecy was *fore*-telling (predictive), but now prophecy shifts strongly to *forth*-telling (exhorting, with elements of faith and patience, etc.). Under the New Testament, the gifts of the Spirit are given as the Spirit wills, and it is our responsibility to follow Him as best we can. Also, on the receiving end of prophecies, a person hearing,

believing, receiving, and complying, all matter in this age of the Church. So, a miss does not constitute a false Prophet, Preacher, or Teacher.

7. **A Prophet is *not* someone who is weird**, wears sackcloth, doesn't bathe very often, and goes around prophesying with a crazed look in their eye, looking for a place to tell what great thing they've "seen" or "heard". Prophets don't get to wander the world without being part of the Body and accountable to it. And they are not exempt from Scriptural accountability from their peers.

8. **A Prophet is not someone who is allowed to deviate from the Word** with an over-emphasis on the Spirit side. Jesus didn't.

Evangelist

Evangelist—a Minister of the Word who brings the gospel to groups of people for the experience of salvation and the establishment of new works, and also who edifies the Church with reminder and motivation toward the Great Commission, usually with healings and miracles.

1. **Salvation and healing to the masses**—an Evangelist is one with a special grace of God to preach the gospel to the masses and bring salvation and healing to multitudes.

2. **Motivation toward the Great Commission**—an Evangelist is given to the Church to keep her ever-motivated toward spreading the gospel of the Lord Jesus Christ and equip every believer to spread the

gospel effectively. Believers benefit from the Evangelist by having their fire kindled, their perspective sharpened, and their destiny reminded.

3. **An Evangelist functions with a definite speaking gift** that captivates, edifies, equips, and lifts a crowd. Evangelists remind believers how happy they are in Christ and how wonderful the simple gospel really is.

4. **Spiritual gifts**—an Evangelist has signs, wonders, miracles, or healings consistently accompanying their preaching.

5. **Compelled toward the lost**—an Evangelist always feels highly compelled to take the gospel to the unreached. And he or she feels the burden of encouraging the Church to do the same. The only named Evangelist in the New Testament was Philip (Acts 21:8), who started as a deacon but then went to Samaria to preach the gospel (Acts 8). Because of the signs, wonders, healings, and deliverances that took place, the people gave heed to Philip and were baptized. Philip then went from town to town with the gospel, awakening people to Christ.

What an Evangelist is *Not*

1. **Leading others to Jesus does not make one an Evangelist**. Because the word "evangelist" means a 'bringer of glad tidings', people have assumed that a Christian who wins souls must certainly be an Evangelist. But that's not right. All Christians are to be filled with the Spirit, have a burden for the lost, and be witnesses, but not all are called to stand in the Office of the Evangelist. There is no "Office of

Soulwinner", and there is no special witnessing "gift" except *the gift of the Holy Spirit* (Acts 1:8). A soulwinner is *any* Christian who obeys Jesus' command to be a witness and tell others the gospel. An Evangelist is something different. Though all Christians can catch "fish" one at a time, and should, Evangelists are equipped with *nets* and a special anointing for a crowd. Many good soulwinners have been under the misconception that they were Evangelists and gone off to start formal ministries without the proper anointing and grace to do it.

2. **Evangelists are not *only* called to convert sinners,** but also have a Church pulpit gift, "And He Himself gave some [to be] apostles, some prophets, some evangelists, and some pastors and teachers, for the equipping of the saints for the work of the ministry, for the edifying of the body of Christ" (Ephesians 4:11-12). Notice that the Evangelist is listed right along with the other Ministers, who are given by Jesus to edify the *Church*—not just sinners. Never forget the value of the Evangelist to the local church crowd *of believers* and not just to crowds of sinners.

Pastor

Pastor—a Minister of the Word who is the shepherd, overseer, nurturer, and "general manager" of the local church assembly.

1. **Definition of a 'Pastor'**—a *shepherd* (Gr. 'poimen'), and therefore is the leader and "manager" of a local assembly and the one most closely connected to the

people of God. The Pastor is one who guides an assembly (a flock) in gospel ministry and Kingdom living, and one who is constantly tending to the people to enhance their spiritual growth and health.

2. **Pastors are feeders of God's Word**, helping "sheep" stay in green pastures and by still waters, being consistently nourished. The Pastor has a clear teaching or preaching gift to consistently edify a local church, and he or she demonstrates an awareness of the spiritual condition of the local saints. The Pastor is the primary one with closest influence and limited authority in a believer's life, aside from the Lord Himself.

3. **Jesus is our model Pastor**—*the Great Shepherd*. Jesus said, "I lay down my life for the sheep" (John 10:15). A good shepherd leads his flock to safety and guards them from predators that seek to hurt them (Gr. 'poimen' is from a root word for *protector*). A good Pastor will give his life for the sheep. If the people know the Pastor has their best interests at heart, they will follow where God leads. A Pastor is caring and watches over the souls of the people (Heb 13:17).

4. **Pastors should pastor supernaturally**, relying on the Holy Spirit to lead them in guiding the people, knowing what to preach and when, recognizing when to correct, rebuke, or address a person, and discerning the needs of the people. They should be able to pick up on some things in the Spirit when necessary, not always being completely surprised when challenges arise and being sharp enough to catch wolves and mark the goats (to be discussed

later). A pastor will have a supernatural ability to counsel and endure with the people.

5. **Spiritual gifts**—Pastors also have signs and wonders accompanying their office, knowing things at times, having power to deliver and heal people and speaking under the inspiration of the Spirit.

6. **Pastors should have a vision to grow their local church assembly.** For the Kingdom to grow in numbers, local churches must grow in numbers. Pastors need to keep in mind what Paul told Timothy, "Do the work of the evangelist" (2 Timothy 4:1-5), and keep the church and the people going after the lost.

7. **Terms for Pastors**—churches use the term "Lead Pastor", "Senior Pastor", "Executive Pastor", or "Associate Pastor", "Care Pastor", "Administrative Pastor" in various ways to denote the function or levels of Pastors at any one church.

8. **Pastors in the early Church**—Aquila and Priscilla (1 Corinthians 16:19), Timothy (also an overseer in Ephesus), Philemon, Apphia, and Archippus (Philemon 1:1-2), and more.

What a Pastor is *Not*

1. **A Pastor is *not* one that has control over people.** Pastors are not dominators of people. Pastors (and all Ministers) are to be loving, humble, and examples to people, "Shepherd the flock of God which is among you, serving as overseers, not by compulsion but willingly, not for dishonest gain but eagerly; nor as being lords over those entrusted to you, but being examples to the flock" (1 Peter 5:2-3). Shepherds

should never be found "lording" over people with force, manipulation, or control.

2. **Pastors will not automatically know *everything* about *everyone*.** Sometimes people are under the impression that God will inform the Pastor supernaturally every time a person is in need or tell the Pastor what everyone's gift is or what everyone should be doing at church. It doesn't work that way.

3. **Pastors are responsible to provide right spiritual substance for people, but they are not responsible for the *outcome*.** The saints have a part in receiving, following, and assimilating right spiritual things into their heart and lifestyle.

4. **Pastors are not the flock's problem solver**—Jesus is. Pastors can only point and guide the sheep to the Lord. Pastors can give the Word and show the solution, but it is Jesus who they must reach.

5. **A Pastor's spouse is not necessarily a co-Pastor.** Some spouses of Pastors may stand in a Ministry Office, but many don't. Therefore, they should not be forced to minister to people in that regard. Certainly, they may love on and minister one on one to people as they feel to, but without the anointing of the Office, they should never be pressured to teach, preach, or counsel in a formal manner.

Teacher

Teacher—a Minister of God's Word who brings clear revelation and assimilation of Bible truths into practical application for believers.

1. **Teachers *explain* the gospel.** (Preachers proclaim the gospel.) Whereas Preachers have a gift to declare a truth and leave it at that, Teachers are more inclined to bring detailed understanding of *why* it's true and how it can be proved Scripturally. Teaching helps people get revelation, whereas preaching helps people get motivation. Both teaching and preaching can cause inspiration. And revelation, motivation, and inspiration are all essential.

2. **Teaching has an impact on people by *assimilating* and *clarifying*** those things written in our heart. (Preaching has an impact on people by swiftly imprinting God's Word in people's hearts.) Teachers are the catalyst for causing understanding and clarity in people about God and His Kingdom.

3. **The Teacher is more focused on the responsibilities of man toward God**, whereas the Preacher's message focuses on declaring what God has done for man. Teachers lay necessary foundations and understanding, detailing our responsibilities first toward God, second toward ourselves, and third toward others (Jones, p. 1).

4. **A good Bible Teacher is one who makes difficult things easy to understand.**

5. **Teachers have a strong desire to see people's faith grow from the revelation they get** from understanding the Word of God. A Teacher's greatest emphasis is explaining the Word of God so people can have a vibrant relationship with the Lord. Gifts of the Spirit and faith with power should be evident in their ministry, confirming the Word they teach.

6. **Teachers mentioned in the early Church**: Simeon, Lucius, and Manaen (Acts 13:1), as well as Paul and Barnabus, who were Apostles as well.

What a Teacher is *Not*

1. **A Teacher is not someone who brings complex, intricate messages that sound "deep"**. Some have made the mistake calling a Teacher "deep" when what he/she teaches is so complicated that it takes three Bible school degrees to understand it. But in reality, a true teaching gift will always take the mysteries of God and make them clearly understandable for *anybody* to get so that they're not mysteries anymore.

2. **The *Office* vs. "gifted to teach"**—The one who stands in the *Office* of Teacher is not just someone who can teach one on one, or in a small class, or on a topic or two, but rather someone who has a grasp of the Word of God in such a way to really help people connect the dots and consistently inspire people to learn more. The local church needs all types who are gifted to teach—classroom teachers, one on one discipleship teachers, and topical teachers.

3. **A Teacher is not necessarily someone who uses a lot of Greek and Hebrew definitions**, a lot of Bible translations, or a lot of historical details. Those things are fine and sometimes effective, but they are not the key attribute of a Teacher's Ministry anointing.

Chapter 3
Other Ministries and Gifts

Though the five Ministry Offices are the primary speakers and premier leaders in the Church, there are many other support ministries and gifts that are necessary to fully edify the Body of Christ.

Deacon

1. **The word 'deacon'** is the Greek word, *diakonos*, which means 'servant', or 'one who executes the commands of another'. Of course, we're all servants of the Lord, so the difference is that we are referring to the "*office* of a deacon", which in today's terms might be a *servant leader*. So, when we speak of church *leaders* under a Minister, many of them are scripturally 'deacons'.

2. **There are qualifications for church leaders.** The first servant leaders of the New Testament were chosen because they were of "good reputation, full of the Holy Spirit and wisdom"(Acts 6:3-5). So that is

paramount. Then we also have 1 Timothy 3:8-12 that gives qualifications for a Deacon:

- reverent
- not double-tongued
- not given to much wine
- not greedy for money
- holding the mystery of the faith with a pure conscience
- tested
- blameless
- husbands of one wife (wives of one husband)
- ruling [their] children and their own houses well

3. **And there is a special promotion for good servant leaders**, "For they that have used the office of a *deacon* well, purchase to themselves a good degree, and great boldness in the faith which is in Christ Jesus" (1 Timothy 3:13). Stephen, one of the first deacons chosen was full of faith and power and "did great wonders and signs among the people" (Acts 6:8). And Philip went to Samaria and did the same thing (Acts 8:5). Stephen was promoted to martyrdom, and Philip was promoted to Evangelist.

4. **Deacons are not the highest authority in a local church**, even if placed on a panel or board. The Pastor should always be the highest authority, getting input from leaders but never "marching orders".

Helps

"And God has appointed these in the church: first apostles, second prophets, third teachers, after that miracles, then gifts of healings, *helps*, administrations, varieties of tongues" (1 Corinthians 12:28).

1. **The *ministry of helps*** is where we find many ministries that aren't specifically mentioned in Scripture. Anything that helps the local church, aides in gospel ministry, or supports any Minister is considered a *help*. It does not refer to persons only, but to the various spiritual gifts which endue men with power to help (Dake, p. 185).

2. **Examples**—musicians, singers, ushers and greeters, children and youth workers (who may or may not actually stand in a Ministry Office), the sound and video team, hospitality, event coordinators, writers, editors, office workers, altar workers, givers, and all the prayers are some examples of *helps*.

3. **The word *helps*** (Gr. 'lempsis' or 'lambono') is *to assist or to support, to help*. One translation uses the term "render loving service" (Weymouth). Operating in the ministry of helps is, indeed, rendering loving service to a church or ministry, to a Pastor or other Minister, and ultimately—most importantly—to the Lord. "For God is not unjust to forget your work and labor of love which you have shown toward His name, in that you have ministered to the saints, and do minister" (Hebrews 6:10).

4. **Oh!**—speaking of the helps ministry would not be complete without Rev. Buddy Bell's powerful charge (quoting Godfrey),

> *Oh! The infinite value of the humble gospel helpers. Thousands of people who have no gifts as leaders are number one —helpers. How grand revival work moves along when red-hot platoons of fired-baptized helpers crowd around God's heroic leaders of the embattled hosts.*

Governments (Administrations)

"And God has appointed these in the church: first apostles, second prophets, third teachers, after that miracles, then gifts of healings, helps, *administrations (governments)*, varieties of tongues" (1 Corinthians 12:28).

1. **The word *administrations*** means 'a steering, a pilot, or governor' (Gr. kubernesis). The word is only used this one time and refers to all the means of coordinating and guidance that happens in the local church. It does not refer to 'power to rule', but to the wisdom and discernment needed to guide a church (Dake, p. 185).

2. ***Administrations* applies to a local church and not to the Church at large**, as there is no organization chart for the worldwide Church (except that Jesus is the Head). Therefore, *governments* would begin with the Pastor, who would be the general manager of the local church, or with the pioneer of a particular local church until such time that it's turned over to a Pastor. And it would continue with the church leaders (deacons), and then with all operations coordination, administration, and functional order of an assembly.

3. **The Ministry Offices do not collectively "govern" the local church.** It is an erroneous teaching to say that Apostles *govern* the sheep while Prophets *guide* the sheep. Rather, *governments* is a particular ministry within the local church or fellowship of churches (notice how governments is listed separately from apostle, prophet, etc.) and includes spiritual and natural coordination (making decisions on volunteers, projects, buying property and equipment, constructing buildings, managing financial affairs, etc.).

Life Gifts and Graces

According to Romans 12:3-8, the Father has graced everyone in some way with some ability that typically seems to flow very naturally and effectively in that person's life. Every believer should recognize what gifting they tend to lean toward and then emphasize it in their life. Even if the person is never called to a Ministry Office or recognized in a formal position, they are still positioned by the Father and are still essential to the building up of the Body of Christ. Here is a brief statement for each. Though all believers should at times have each of these, some are just more prone to them than others, and there they find their place in the Body of Christ.

1. **Some are given to *prophecy*** in that they speak with forthrightness, insight, and the ability to influence (They may also be more open to the special

manifestation of prophecy, but not necessarily stand in a Ministry Office.)

2. **Some are given to *ministry***, in that they render loving service to meet the needs of others.

3. **Some are given to *teach***—not necessarily to stand in the Ministry Office of Teacher, but to instruct effectively.

4. **Some are given to *exhort***, by making an appeal to people to comfort, encourage, or edify them.

5. **Some are prone to *giving***, with a spirit of generosity and liberality with their resources. All believers should give, but some have special grace in it.

6. **Some are prone to *lead***, "standing in front", being an example, and coordinating church activities.

7. **Some are great *mercy givers***, sympathizing with the others, suffering long, and bearing others' burdens with compassion.

One way to look at it is that all three of the Godhead are involved in the giving of gifts. God gives the life graces and sets the operations, Jesus gives the Offices, and the Holy Spirit gives the manifestations / gifts. This notes the involvement of each member of the Trinity in the completion of the work. Each member of the *Godhead* is needed. And in turn, each member of the *Body of Christ* is needed. Every believer should recognize what gifting they tend to lean toward and then emphasize it and work to develop it in their life.

Gifts of the Spirit (Manifestations)

The gifts of the Spirit are given to help others and build the Church. Scripturally, they are called *manifestations of the Spirit*, and they are only given as the Spirit wills. "...the *manifestation* of the Spirit is given to each one for the profit of all" (1 Corinthians 12:7-10). Every Ministry Office comes equipped with an anointing for one or more of these manifestations (frequent or occasional), and all believers who are filled with the Spirit should begin to experience one or several of these manifestations given by the Spirit. All of these manifestations require faith to step out and act. And no one actually owns or possesses any gift permanently, but rather is "used by God" when the Spirit manifests a gift for a moment.

There are nine of these gifts. Three of them *say* something, three of them *do* something, and three of them *reveal* something. We are commanded to desire the best gifts (1 Corinthians 12:31). Though some of the gifts seem a bit more dramatic than others, the best gift is really the one needed the most at any moment of time. And very often these manifestations occur together.

Our desire for the gifts to manifest, our faith to use them for the benefit of people, and the actual need for the gifts play an important part in the Holy Spirit manifesting them. Also, learning to yield and to cooperate with the Spirit of God is important to operate in the gifts. Holiness affects the gifts, as the purer the vessel, the purer the gift. And love is the catalyst for it all. Even our use in the gifts must be motivated by love, wanting to simply help people and never for personal gain or glory.

There is not a lot of instruction on the revelation or power gifts in the Scripture because if the Holy Spirit does not give the gift, you can't initiate it—unlike the utterance gifts, which can be initiated by the human will even if no manifestation present. Therefore, there is ample instruction given in the Scriptures in relation to the utterance gifts (1 Corinthians 14) so that they are not abused.

The Revelation Gifts

1. **Word of Wisdom**—the supernatural revelation by the Spirit of God concerning only a part of the divine purpose and plan in the mind of God. The word of wisdom is a *foretelling*—informing us about something that is going to happen—certain facts about the future—to man that give insight into a certain outcome. The word of wisdom is always future tense—that which is yet unborn: hidden things we would not normally or naturally know. There is no "gift" of wisdom, but only a brief *word* of wisdom. And it is not *natural* wisdom, or even *spiritual* wisdom, but a momentary *special* wisdom that gives insight into a certain outcome. *Bible examples*: Agabus knowing of the coming drought (Acts 11:28), Paul knowing he was to witness in Rome (Acts 23:11), Agabus knowing Paul would be imprisoned (Acts 21:11), Paul knowing of the coming shipwreck (Acts 27:10).

2. **Word of Knowledge**—a supernatural revelation by the Spirit of certain facts in the mind of God about

the present or past, with the purpose of helping someone. This has nothing to do with being educated or scholastic, profound knowledge of God's Word, or intimate knowledge of God, which we can all have; but rather a momentary gift of the Spirit to reveal a beneficial fact about something or someone that would otherwise remain hidden. *Bible examples*: Jesus knowing the adulterous woman at the well (John 4:16-18), Ananias knowing where Saul would be (Acts 9:10-11), Peter knowing the two had lied to the Holy Spirit (Acts 5:1-4), Peter knowing three men had come to see him (Acts 10:17-19).

3. **Discerning of Spirits**—gives supernatural insight into the spirit world, being able to perceive by seeing or hearing into the spirit realm to detect angels, demons, or see the condition of human spirits. This gift has nothing to do with having good discernment and judgment about things, as all Christians can know when something is true or false, right or wrong, good or evil, error in teaching, etc. And it has nothing to do with a power to find faults in others or read minds. But it refers to a brief moment of the Holy Spirit allowing a person to see, detect, or know of spirits present, thus providing comfort, help, or deliverance for someone. *Bible examples:* when Jesus met the Gadarenian demoniac and heard the demon speak (Mark 5:1-10), Paul perceived the demon was harassing him and cast it out (Acts 16:18), John seeing the Lord and the Spirit(s) of God (Revelation 4:5), Jesus knowing Nathanael was a pure Israelite (John 1:47).

The Power Gifts

4. **Faith**—a special, momentary faith that surpasses any and all doubt for the purpose of working a miracle, healing the sick, delivering the oppressed, raising the dead, or receiving a mighty miracle. This is not the measure of faith that we all have and that we all are to be increasing in to trust God more deeply, and it is not saving faith, but rather a momentary faith that comes on a person and then lifts after a work is done. It is almost like a cloak of invincibility placed on someone to empower them to do a mighty work or carry them through to a mighty miracle. *Bible examples:* Peter raised Tabitha from the dead (Acts 9:36-42), Peter was able to sleep the night before his execution (Acts 12:6-11), and probably more.

5. **Gifts of Healings**—a special manifestation of God's power to heal a sick person. This is not the medical profession or anything to do with natural remedies or expertise, but a supernatural momentary power to eliminate a disease, sometimes working in conjunction with other gifts. This is not regular faith for healing, but an anointing for healing at certain times. It is plural, referring to how different persons may have different graces to heal particular diseases rather than one gift to heal everything. *Bible examples:* Jesus healed the deaf mute with spit and fingers in his ears (Mark 7:31-36), Jesus healed the blind man using spit in his eyes (Mark 8:22-23), Peter and John healed the man at the gate (Acts 3:1-16).

6. **Working of Miracles**—a manifestation in a moment, causing supernatural things to happen for

people by a command, a declaration, or an action of faith. A miracle is not something natural like the sun rising and setting or the birth of a baby, but rather it is the supernatural intervention into the ordinary course of nature. *Bible examples:* Jesus turned water into wine (John 2), Jesus fed the multitudes (Matthew 14:13-21), Jesus put the ear back on the soldier (Luke 22:49-51).

The Utterance Gifts

7. **Prophecy**—divinely inspired utterance, speaking forth words of God (thoughts, intents, purposes) by the Holy Spirit with the purpose of blessing and encouraging people. Prophecy brings edification and exhortation and comfort to men (1 Corinthians 14:3). To edify is to build up or strengthen. To exhort is to encourage or call nearer to God or to invite and advise. To comfort is a coming along side to give strength, bring peace, cheer up, or console. The Greek word for 'prophesy' means *to speak for another*, meaning the gift is given to speak for God. This is *forthtelling*—not *foretelling*, and has nothing to do with predicting the future (which is covered by the word of wisdom). It is not just a leading of the Spirit to speak something from your own spirit, but rather a divine utterance from the Holy Spirit. It is not the general *spirit of prophecy*, which is the testimony of Jesus (Revelation 19:10). And it is not given for correction or conviction. Though there can sometimes be an element of prophecy in God-inspired teaching or preaching, the actual *manifestation* of prophecy only comes by unction of

the Spirit and is to arrest people's attention by clearly being God speaking through someone.

8. **Tongues**—supernatural manifestation of languages of men or of angels. This is not being an educated linguist or speaking multiple known languages, but an ability to speak in an unknown tongue from our spirit as the Spirit gives utterance, where our mind is not involved and doesn't comprehend. This gift manifests in the midst of an assembly of people (two or more), but only if an interpretation is also given. The purpose is the same as prophecy—to relay a fresh message from Heaven to bless and encourage those who are present. It is also possible that the tongue is in a known language to one of the hearers and for the same purpose (Acts 2:11). (The personal use of divers tongues in private prayer is not considered one of these nine gifts of the Spirit, as these are only given *as the Spirit wills* and almost exclusively for the blessing of *others*, whereas *praying* in tongues is for ourselves and can be done without waiting on the Spirit to initiate it—1 Corinthians 14:4-17.)

9. **Interpretation of Tongues**—a momentary manifestation of the Spirit to interpret what someone has just spoken in an unknown tongue. It isn't a translation of the tongue, but rather is an *interpretation* of the tongue that gives forth the meaning. The purpose is to bless and encourage those who are present with a fresh word from God. Tongues with interpretation basically *equals* prophecy. Could a person have a tongue and an interpretation in their private prayer time alone?

Possibly, but the manifestation is primarily experienced with others.

Chapter 4
A Minister's Responsibility

What is *real* gospel ministry? What is the *real* assignment and priority for those in a Ministry Office? This should not be left up to personal preference, desire, or opinion. But it must come from *Scripture* alone if a Minister is to be solid, anchored, and fully pleasing to the Lord.

Our Scriptural Assignment

> And He gave [gifts to men—Ministers] ...for the equipping of the saints for the work of the ministry, for the edifying of the Body of Christ, till we all come to the unity of the faith and of the knowledge of the Son of God, to a perfect man, to the measure of the stature of the fullness of Christ; that we should no longer be children, tossed to and fro and carried about with every wind of doctrine, by the trickery of men, in the cunning craftiness of deceitful plotting, but speaking the truth in love, may grow up in all things into Him who is the head—

Christ—from whom the whole Body, joined and knit together by what every joint supplies, according to the effective working by which every part does its share, causes growth of the Body for the edifying of itself in love (Ephesians 4:11-16).

1. **The growth of the Body**—Ministers are given to build the Church and edify and equip the saints—nothing more and nothing less.

2. **Leading the Church**—under the Lordship of Christ, Ministers are responsible for the direction of the Church, so we must have the Lord's heart concerning it. We are responsible for the right and only gospel being spread effectively. In whatever territory of the Kingdom we are in, we are the examples, and what we do matters. Leading people is a great responsibility. Great responsibility requires great wisdom. So, Ministers must pursue God's wisdom until that *spirit of wisdom* abides on them (Ephesians 1:17, Isaiah 11:2).

3. **Ministers are *stewards of the mysteries* of God**, "Let a man so consider us, as servants of Christ and stewards of the mysteries of God. Moreover it is required in stewards that one be found faithful" (1 Corinthians 4:1-2). God has entrusted Ministers with the Word of God concerning the New Covenant as given by the Spirit through the heart of Jesus. Ministers have no business preaching any other gospel. The health of the Church is dependent on the spiritual food that Ministers provide.

4. ***Speaking** to people also includes responsibility to people*. It's all about people. It's *not* about the

Minister. We have a responsibility to Minister in purity and accuracy.

5. **Jesus is the Head**—the decisions we make, the way we lead the people, the example we set, and the things we preach must be God's will. We're responsible to keep our ministry to people in step with the *Word of God* rather than blindly follow our gospel upbringing, our familiar traditions, or our favorite television preachers. It may seem sometimes that the gospel is just a bunch of people propagating random personal preferences, but it should not be so since we have a Lord.

6. **Ministers are not given to the *world*, but to the *Church*.** New Testament gospel ministry demands that we emphasize Spirit-filled disciple making and imparting God's Word and Spirit into the hearts of believers. There is nothing in the job description set forth above about leading community charges or political campaigns, fighting society's immorality, focusing on the Middle East, or getting entangled in world affairs. The whole Church has a "voice to the world", but it's not an Old Testament message of judgment and threat, but rather the New gospel message of salvation through Jesus Christ. A Minister's attention is to be on the Church, discipling the people of God and bringing new believers into the fold. We build the Church—not nations, cities, or secular communities. Our Office is higher than a political office, so while it's a dishonor to neglect our civic duties, it's also a dishonor to combine our Minister call with a natural, political one. We have authority to deal with *Church* morality rather than *world* morality.

Preachers are to affect the *saved*, so that the *saved* can affect the *unsaved*. Those other things may be someone's personal interest or vocation, but they are not part of a Minister's call or responsibility (according to Scripture) and should be kept separate from gospel ministry. Of course we vote, and we teach the people the right gospel perspective on social and secular issues so they can vote Biblically and "answer every man" with wisdom. It's just that if we're not careful, secular efforts and reactionary preaching can crowd out our Scriptural assignment. And worldly political affairs rarely cause people to be more compassionate toward the lost, but only more cynical.

7. **How the world sees us vs. the Truth**—the world views Ministers as those who do weddings, funerals, soup kitchens, community rallies, Christmas services, and Easter plays. Those outward things are the only way for unsaved, non-spiritual people to relate to the things of God. But according to Scripture, those are not our priorities. Ministers are given to the Church to preach God's Word and raise up mature believers who exemplify Christ. The world has no idea of the holy thing we are called to, so don't buy into majoring on the minors. Ministers are responsible to create a Kingdom culture with a focus that is not influenced by the world.

8. **Ministers are examples**—"Be an example to the believers in word, in conduct, in love, in spirit, in faith, in purity" (1 Timothy 4:12). Ministers are to live and preach the Great Commission and the great commandment. Ministers must keep this in mind at all times, never wanting to cause anyone to stumble

because of their spiritual carelessness. Be all things to all people, so that you can win some (1 Corinthians 9:22).

Understanding the Church at Large

1. **How does Church edification take place?** It happens primarily in the local church service setting with all that takes place therein, along with special meetings, conferences, campmeetings, Bible schools, one-on-one, and more. And it happens through Bibles, books, television, audio, video, and internet media. All are valid and necessary for a Christian and the Church to grow. With all of the gospel spreading tools at our disposal, we have a responsibility to make full use of them to reach and teach people.

2. **The local church assembly is God's idea,** and it's His heartbeat. The Greek word for *Church* is Ekklesia, which means 'assembly of called out ones'. This means that rather than it being our own idea to meet together, God has actually *called us out*, summoning us out of our homes to congregate frequently and consistently, and even more frequently as we see the Day approaching (Hebrews 10:25). The local church assembly is where people get planted by the Lord (Psalm 92:12-14) and where holy things happen. It is where the Lord has placed a shepherd and a structure to care for people's spiritual life on a regular basis. The Christian life is not just our own private affair. To be a real disciple of Christ, it's necessary to be not only a radical believer sold out to

Jesus, but also a sincerely committed church member in a local assembly sharing in its worship, its fellowship, and its witness.

Certainly, we belong to the Universal Church ("the general assembly and church of the firstborn ...whose names are written in heaven" (Hebrews 12:32). But that's not all. We must belong to some local branch of it. Over 80% of the use of the word 'church' in the New Testament is referring to the local assembly. The local church is where disciples come together to worship together, pray together, serve together, contribute together, sharpen one another, build friendships centered around Jesus, and learn and grow together. The local church is where we go consistently, week to week, which allows us to develop responsibility, commitment, and faithfulness to God and others. Without consistent assembly, believers will not develop their love walk nor grow relationally with other brothers and sisters in Christ. And they will not remain spiritually healthy and mature.

"Lampstands" are a holy thing. Jesus sent letters to seven local churches (Revelation 1-3, seven golden lampstands), instructing the Pastor of each in spiritual matters of correction and encouragement. Jesus expects us to be assembled together (Hebrews 10:25), for it is His Body. No one person is bigger than a "lampstand".

God's Word instructs to not forsake or neglect the assembling of ourselves together (Hebrews 10:25). So, we must esteem the local church very highly. Bible schools and great teaching ministries provide essential gospel training, but with the purpose of sending people back to grow local churches or pioneer them. Each local church is a living, breathing unit of the Body. And it is very special to God.

3. **Special meetings**—conventions, conferences, "campmeetings", and other special meetings provide great complement to the believer's growth. Having multiple and consecutive meetings provides an acceleration for spiritual development. These special meetings are usually focused on a certain theme that causes a level of expectancy and excitement to trigger people's faith. They also give people exposure to other ministries and broaden people's vision and hope for life and Church, and they can provide a means for specially inviting the unsaved or the unlearned.

4. **Bible schools**—good Bible schools and training centers provide quick and thorough education for believers and Ministers. Bible schools can be either part of a church or a separate ministry altogether, and they usually exist for the two-fold purpose of 1) sending trained believers back to their home churches to serve and lead, and 2) sending Ministers around the world to preach, teach, and start new works. One added benefit of Bible schools is the heightened spiritual climate where a unified hunger, excitement, and purpose are prevalent.

5. **Don't despise one or the others.** All ministries and Ministers are important to the Body. Don't fall into the trap of comparing ministries, or you'll begin to "hate the one and love the other, or else he will be loyal to the one and despise the other" (Luke 16:13).

In this day of worldwide gospel organizations and television ministries that are huge in scope and impact, there's a tendency to glorify the big ministries as heroes and belittle the local church unless it is a mega-church. Much of it has to do with familiarity, where week after week, we're close to the same people and the same Pastor and same things which can begin to seem a bit mundane. But to God it is not so. Value the local church and the Pastors.

On the other hand, don't despise the outside ministries who are providing an essential part of the discipleship process. Pastors should not discourage people from going to Bible schools and special meetings outside the local church.

6. **Keep the Church at large in mind**—Ministers should work together. Pastors should look to bring other Ministers to preach to the people, recognizing not only the value of the different anointing and grace of the other Offices, but also the fact that people usually respond well to a Preacher they haven't been hearing every week. It may increase the chance for miracles or it may open up people for revelation. It could be new revelation, or it could be the same exact concepts the Pastors have conveyed, yet the people hear it fresh and the light comes on in them. And it's all about the people. Pastors shouldn't be intimidated or insecure about people enjoying and gleaning from the other Gifts.

Traveling Ministers should be careful to make good relationships with Pastors and attempt to do much of their ministry in the local churches. They should look at it as supporting the Pastor who is shepherding the people, being careful to not plow the Pastor's field crosswise but keep unity and consistency for the people's sake. Meetings held outside the local church setting should not be purposed to gather a following and pull people from their local church assembly, but rather to support the people in their growth and send them back to their local assembly with more fire than before. It would go a long way for Ministers holding outside meetings or television ministries to remind the people to get planted or stay planted in a local church assembly so that they aren't "couch Christians" or scattered sheep without fellowship and leadership.

Don't steal sheep. Never injure one local church to build another or be so caught up in your own thing that you realize you're pulling people from where they are planted. Teach the people to not steal sheep either. If the church someone is in is dangerous or completely off track, a gentle invite for better "spiritual food" may be appropriate. But keep the Church 'at large' in mind.

7. **Points of caution**—the local church sometimes feels the negative effect of routine, while outside meetings sometimes feel the negative effect of a lack of unity and lack of continuance. Whereas some traveling Ministers provide enthusiasm and sometimes have a seemingly larger and exciting niche ministry, the Pastors provide consistency and nurturing that the others don't, and are responsible to give the whole counsel of God rather than a targeted niche. Conferences and conventions tend to swiftly awaken and refresh people with a style of meeting and

ministry that is revolutionary and necessary for every believer. It just can't happen every week.

For Bible schools, the point of caution is to realize that the heightened spiritual climate is not real life, as once school is over and you're out in the trenches, it may feel totally different. For example, at school, you're with two hundred people who are hungry for God and worshipping with all their heart, but then God sends you to start a church where thirty five people assemble the first year, fifteen of which are only partially interested.

8. **One option for certain Ministers who sense a call is to serve the local church they're in.** They don't necessarily need to launch out with a traveling ministry, but should help the Church at large by offering to impart their niche ministry within the local church, take on some of the Pastoral responsibilities, or facilitate discipleship in some way.

> Some who are called to the Ministry are looking for something greater than the local church because they don't see the greatness of the local church. There's much routine in a church family, and those with ideas of grandeur aren't looking for routine. They don't realize that in the routine lies the secret of greatness and success.
>
> —Pastor Nancy Dufresne

9. **A great picture of the local church** is seen in Acts 2:42-47, where the people were together in fellowship, in eating together, in prayers, and in full support of each other. They were together daily either in the temple or breaking bread from house to

house. And they praised God together. In every local church, there should be the large congregational setting (or *corporate* setting). And in every local church, there should be the smaller group setting where the saints get to fellowship and love one another more closely. Since the goal of every local church is to spread the gospel and grow, once it gets too big for the intimate fellowship atmosphere, it should have a plan to provide and encourage the smaller group setting for their people. If it doesn't, the people will miss the part of their spiritual development and health that only vibrant relationships can provide.

10. **"Para-church ministries"**, such as orphanages, prison ministries, homeless ministries, and other care ministries have one of two approaches. Either they are set up like a local church, where people meet regularly for fellowship and serving one another and with a Pastor to teach and nurture them. Or they are more of an evangelistic outreach from a local church, where the people might not even be saved yet or interested in God more than getting the natural help. In any case, for the Ministers of these, remember that your Scriptural assignment is to lead people to Jesus and disciple them spiritually more than it is to feed and clothe them. As a Christian, we feed and clothe and care for them naturally when we have opportunity. But as a Minister, our assignment is to help them develop spiritually.

The Care of People

1. **Ministers carry people.** We carry them in our hearts. We care for their well being and their success in life. We care for the unity and love within the local church congregation. We are responsible to *watch over their souls and give account one day* (Hebrews 13:17). And that can be heavy at times. Paul mentioned it in his list of Ministry hardships, "Beside those things that are without, that which cometh upon me daily, *the care of all the churches*" (2 Corinthians 11:28). This goes for more than just the Pastors—all Ministers should accept the care for and responsibility to people. A preacher who has no real desire for people, but only for a distant exchange of "ministry for money", is not a very good person.

2. **Ministers give themselves to people.** They belong to people, "Therefore let no man glory in men. For all things are yours; Whether Paul, or Apollos, or Cephas, or the world, or life, or death, or things present, or things to come; all are yours" (1 Corinthians 3:21-22). On the gospel ministry front, Ministers are given to the people, who get to "open Ministers up" (as a gift) for spiritual help and blessing.

3. **Pure Ministers pour their hearts and souls out for the people**, "So being affectionately desirous of you, we were willing to have imparted unto you, not the gospel of God only, but *also our own souls*, because ye were dear unto us" (1 Thessalonians 2:8). That's why we feel so raw and exposed after preaching. It's not because of the scriptures we quoted. It's because of the personal honesty and heart sharing, where our

soul opened up to them. And our soul is quite sensitive in this spirit to spirit gospel exchange.

4. **Ministers don't point people to themselves to gain a following.** Ministers point people to Jesus because it's all about connecting them to God. Spiritual people can always detect when the Preacher actually cares about them versus when the Preacher is just showing off intellect or transfixing you on their viewpoint, or where it's all about making a name for themselves. High achievers are interested in other people and care about them. Low achievers are not interested in others, but inward focused. A self-centered Minister will never take the people very far in the Lord.

5. **Keep the cares cast over on God.** Christians are to bear each other's burdens (Galatians 6:2). But Ministers are not called to bear *everybody's* burdens. Jesus said "My burden is light and My yoke is easy." So, be sure to let Jesus carry the heavier end. Cast all your care upon the Lord.

6. **Help people all you can, but don't get entangled in their personal problems.** You can't help people out of a pit if you jump in with them, but only if you stay on top and throw the rope. Give them the truth. Give them the power of God. Give them compassion. But as a Minister, don't let someone else's chaos get inside you, "...each one shall bear his own load" (Galatians 6:5).

Instant In Season and Out

"I charge you in the presence of God and of Christ Jesus...Preach the word; be ready (instant) in season and out of season; reprove, rebuke, and exhort, with complete patience and teaching" (2 Timothy 4:1-2).

1. **Instant and ready—what does it mean?** It means ministering when you don't want to—when you're tired, when you're sick, when you don't feel spiritual, when you've just had a "discussion" with your spouse on the way to church, when you're going through hardship, when you're just not in the mood, and *when it doesn't feel like you have anything to give to anyone.* The Holy Spirit will always show up if you will take your position by faith. Minister your heart out under the anointing, and then you may go back to your circumstance afterward. The Lord and the people are counting on you.

   Lester Sumrall said, "God uses me *because I live ready.*"

2. **Ministers must be consistent and *findable*.** Ministry is all about people counting on you. Ministers don't hide from the people. Ministers don't skip church. So, Ministers should schedule all of their interruptions during non-service times. The gospel that we are entrusted with takes priority. The thing can wait. The family can wait. Show the family how to fit everything in, but only around church and gospel. For example, celebrate the birthday the day before, after, or between the two hours where people

have come together in the Lord. Let the extreme emergencies be the exception. This goes for traveling Preachers, too. Traveling Preachers should be faithfully connected to a local church and be there when they're not on the road. They need the assembly, and the assembly needs them.

3. **This does not mean that Ministers can never say "No"** to someone who is wanting their time. Certainly, we must first follow the Spirit and make wise decisions about how our time is spent. And certainly, we should have our safe zones and personal times when we are unreachable.

Recognize the Need for All Offices

1. **Like spokes on a wheel or fingers on a hand, all five Ministry Offices are essential** for a flock to be healthy. No one gift, however eloquent or powerful, is enough to complete the development of any one Christian. Jesus gave five. We need all five. Don't prefer or exalt any one above another. It doesn't mean that every church must have all five Gifts resident in their assembly, but it does mean those Gifts should be passing through occasionally to impart into the people.

2. **Ministers should recognize the need for one another** and work together toward the same goal of perfecting the Body. Pastors should make effort to let other Ministers preach to the people. Other Ministers should look to do most of their work in

the local church, working with the Pastor since that's where the sheep live.

3. **Sharing the Ministry**—Pastors should be willing to share some local church *resources*. The other Ministers should find a way to share some local church *responsibilities*. This obviously implies some sharing of *vision*, which requires a collaborative effort between Ministers.

Expect Some Hardship

1. **Ministry includes hardship**. Part of being entrusted with the power of God and this great gospel is the encounter with certain suffering, "That I may know him, and the power of his resurrection, and the fellowship of his sufferings" (Philippians 3:10). Though many Ministers will avoid stripes and imprisonments, you will certainly need to expect the other things in Paul's list:

> But in all [things] we commend ourselves as ministers of God: in much patience, in tribulations, in needs, in distresses, in stripes, in imprisonments, in tumults, in labors, in sleeplessness, in fastings; by purity, by knowledge, by longsuffering, by kindness, by the Holy Spirit, by sincere love, by the word of truth, by the power of God, by the armor of righteousness on the right hand and on the left, by honor and dishonor, by evil report and good report; as deceivers, and [yet] true; as unknown and [yet] well known; as dying, and behold we live; as chastened, and [yet] not killed; as

sorrowful, yet always rejoicing; as poor, yet making many rich; as having nothing, and [yet] possessing all things (2 Corinthians 6:4-10).

2. **The illusion of American Ministry "luxury" is not the norm.** Pure Ministers should be mentally and spiritually prepared for ministry *anywhere*, even in nations where Christians are being persecuted and killed, and be willing to go if the Lord calls.

3. **The hard part is not the pulpit time.** The hard part is the people issues side. God chooses us knowing who can handle the people side and patiently deal with people's difficulties, solve conflicts amongst church members, and sacrifice their own comfort to "warn those who are unruly, comfort the fainthearted, uphold the weak, be patient with all" (1 Thessalonians 5:14). The teaching, preaching, and ministry time isn't the sacrifice. It's the ministry life and people management side, making important decisions regarding the Body of Christ.

4. **Be tough.** Persevere. Endure. Don't be emotional. Live by the ascendency of your spirit rather than the emotions of your soul. Pure Ministers are to be undeterred by hardship and formidable against all the devil's threats. Paul said, "For I am ready not only to be bound, but also to die at Jerusalem for the name of the Lord Jesus" (Acts 21:13).

The Ministry is not a life of holy ecstasy with a beautiful halo, a heavenly time, a ride in a limousine. It is a desperate struggle, a terrific experience. "For I will show him how many things he must suffer for My name's sake" (Acts 9:16).

If I were pledging men and women to the gospel of the Son of God...it would not be to have a nice church and harmonious surroundings and a sweet do nothing time. I would invite them to be ready to die...John Wesley established a heroic call....He demanded every preacher to be ready to pray, ready to preach, ready to die. That is always the spirit of Christianity. When there is any other spirit that comes into the Church, it is not the spirit of Christianity (Lake, p. 101, 105).

Chapter 5
Ministry Preparation that Pleases God

Preparation to stand in a Ministry Office is no small matter, it doesn't happen accidentally, and it requires diligence. Jesus spent thirty years in preparation. Paul the Apostle spent his youth training under the Old Covenant and then thirteen or fourteen years in preparation before his Apostleship. And the twelve Apostles were trained personally by Jesus for three and a half years.

One requirement for a Ministry Office is that he's "not a novice, lest being lifted up with pride he fall into the same condemnation as the devil" (1 Timothy 3:6). Though God will never take back a call or a gift (Romans 11:29), He absolutely expects His Ministers to have certain qualities, sincere commitment, and honed spiritual skills. And many times, though a person is called and gifted, they are not placed into an Office until those things are secure, sometimes many years later. Preparation time is never wasted time.

Consecration

> I believe that God's ministers are to be flames of fire. Nothing less than flames. Nothing less than mighty instruments with burning messages, with hearts full of love. They must have a depth of consecration that God has taken full charge of the body and it exists only that it may manifest the glory of God.
>
> —Smith Wigglesworth

1. **The best Ministers are those who have truly forsaken all**, "who when he had found one pearl of great price, went and sold all that he had and bought it" (Matthew 13:46). Real Preachers are *total gospel people*. Their life centers around Jesus and spreading His Word. A Preacher's life is to spend and be spent to bring light to a dark world and to prepare others for the same. They are fully committed to God and people, even before they stand in an Office. It means giving up our need for status, popularity, money, pursuits, and personal dreams. And it means giving up the world.

2. **Ministers become a "gazing stock" to the world.** We give up our old persona and become the "city set on a hill" for all to see. For all the Christian commands to not be a stumbling-block, to not be unequally yoked with unbelieving friends, to not be entangled in the world, and so on, how much more for the Minister? "No one engaged in warfare entangles himself with the affairs of this life, that he may please him who enlisted him as a soldier " (2 Timothy 2:4).

3. **Touching spirit**—the only effective ministry is that which is spirit to spirit. For a Minister, it is imperative that people can touch your spirit. And the only way for that to happen is if your flesh, your emotions, and your *self* is purged and gone. If your outward man is too strong and stubborn with pride or self preservation, your inward man cannot reach past it to help people.

   Catch the personal attitude of Paul, "I have been crucified with Christ; it is no longer I who live, but Christ lives in me; and the *life* which I now live in the flesh I live by faith in the Son of God, who loved me and gave Himself for me" (Galatians 2:20). When *self* reaches *zero*, we are ready. That means a lot of character chiseling might be required between the call and the answer.

4. **Egg shells**—if people are continually having to walk on "egg shells" around you to not offend you, anger you, or hurt your feelings, it is a sign that something of your *self* is not crucified and your feelings are out on your shoulder. This puts people and the Ministry in jeopardy. And you're not yet ready.

Commitment for a Lifetime

1. **Count the cost, because it's for life.** "For which of you, intending to build a tower, does not sit down first and count the cost, whether he has enough to finish it" (Luke 14:27-28). Answering a true call to a Ministry Office is different than taking a job somewhere that you know can leave at any time if

you don't like the scene. A Ministry call is *who you are*, and you won't be able to run from it and stay happy. You'll need unwavering faith to make the decision and set your course, and you'll need unwavering faith to keep that course for the rest of your life. No matter the difficulties, no matter the disappointments, no matter the circumstances—your faith and commitment must remain.

2. **No excuses**—Many have been called, but the uncertainty of Ministry life and the lack of total commitment hinders them. They make big promises for later, they delay because of natural circumstances, and they look back (Luke 9:57-62). When Elijah threw his mantle on Elisha, Elisha burned his "bridge" so he couldn't go back. He was in his trade, plowing with oxen, but took a couple of those oxen, killed and cooked them, and had a final feast with his family. The key to it was that the wood he used for the cooking fire was his plowing equipment, symbolizing his leaving his old life for his new calling. He didn't keep a "look back crutch" (1 Kings 19:19-21).

3. **Christians need longevity—Ministers even more so.** Real Preachers don't quit or retire. Once you're called, that calling will burn in you until the last day. Maybe your season transitions to a different grace or final phase, but you will always be preaching somehow because people need the gift. Plan on it. Longevity and consistency creates stability for the Kingdom and for Christians, so endure and stay "all in" until the end.

Passing the Tests

1. **To step into and advance in our calling, we'll need to pass the tests.** God *never* tests anyone with evil—with sickness, with tragedy, or with temptation to sin and get out of the will of God (James 1). However, God certainly *does* test us with words, commands, questions, and assignments. "And you shall remember that the Lord your God led you all the way these forty years in the wilderness, *to humble you and test* you, to know what was in your heart, whether you would keep His commandments or not" (Deuteronomy 8:2). God searches the heart and tries the reins (Jeremiah 17:10). Philip was faithful as a deacon and took initiative after being scattered, and God opened to him doors to evangelize (Acts 8).

2. **Assignments**—there will be some key assignments and some hard to understand assignments that you must get right, or you won't be promoted. "If you are willing and obedient, you shall eat the good of the land" (Isaiah 1:19). Notice that you must be willing *and* obedient. You can't just grudgingly give in and obey God. You must get *willing*, and for as long as it takes. Always go where God sends you and give your best always.

3. **Faith**—the Word says that the "just shall live by faith" (Romans 1:17, Galatians 3:11, Hebrews 10:38). Ministers should expect to face many tests of faith as they approach their first phase or subsequent phases of Ministry. Not all the tests will be from God (some will be from the world or from

the devil), but God will be watching to see if you're able to hear from Him before making a move, if you've learned to trust Him completely for your needs and see miracles happen, if you're unafraid of all challenges, if you're unashamed of the gospel, if you're undaunted by demons, and if you've overcome the world and the devil, "I write to you, young men, because you have overcome the wicked one" (1 John 2:13). God tests your faithfulness. He tests your motives. He examines your endurance and your resolve to see if your obedience is unwavering and can be trusted. He wants you to have some wins on your record so your strength is secure.

4. **It is God who promotes**, "For promotion cometh neither from the east, nor from the west, nor from the south. But God is the judge: he putteth down one, and setteth up another" (Psalm 75:6-7, KJV). At each season, recognize what phase of Ministry you are in. Find and function in your own office and anointing. Protect it. Do it faithfully. Develop it. Study and be active. Take it seriously and be diligent. It's not other Ministers that initiate your promotion, but God. So be patient, and serve the Lord.

5. **Stability before Office**—God is looking for Ministers to be stable in life, stable in mind and emotion, and stable in identity. Until your love walk is "smooth and deep", you're not ready. A title doesn't carry much weight without the Godliness to sustain it.

Mastering God's Word

1. **God's written Word is where it all begins.** You must build your ministry on the Word of God—not on the supernatural and not on a gift. Ministers should always remain grounded in the Word and sharp in the Truth, or their ministry will eventually falter. The Word of God is to be our focus. It's the only thing to preach.

2. **Honor the Word. Value the Word. Esteem the Word.** The Word is the first authority. It is the final authority. Without it, we have no authority. Not even the Spirit can perform without the Word. He will never contradict anything that's already been written by God.

   > Never compare the word of God with other books. Comparisons are dangerous. Never think or say that this book *contains* the Word of God. It *is* the Word of God. It is supernatural in origin, eternal in duration, inexpressible in value, infinite in scope, regenerative in power, infallible in authority, universal in interest, personal in application, inspired in totality. Read it through. Write it down. Pray it in. Work it out. And then pass it on. And truly the Word of God changes a man until he becomes an epistle of God.
   >
   > —Smith Wigglesworth

3. **There are few things in Ministry more disheartening than a Minister who doesn't know his Bible.** Those being preached to are counting on the Truth and nothing but the Truth. "Be diligent to

present yourself approved to God, a worker who does not need to be ashamed, rightly dividing the word of truth" (2 Timothy 2:15). For a "man of God [to] be complete, thoroughly equipped for every good work", it requires *all Scripture* (2 Timothy 3:16-17). Esteem the Word in your personal life and in your preparation. You should expect to know your Bible better than the people you preach to and better than every naysayer.

4. **Stay fresh in the Word**, reading the Bible for more than just to prepare a teaching or sermon. Faith and revelation in your heart are necessary for success, and they only come from the Word of God.

5. **Emphasize the New Testament more than the Old.** And don't feel guilty about it. God is the one who decided to make a New one and make the Old one obsolete. The New Covenant is better, and it's God's absolute favorite (Hebrews 8:6-13). It's not that the Old is completely irrelevant, but that it must be interpreted through the blood of Jesus, just as the early Apostles did as they preached the gospel and recorded the New Testament using scriptures from the Old Testament. The Apostles figured it out—that the cross of Jesus Christ changed everything. So, either you and I can try and repeat their effort of unraveling of the mystery to explain the doctrine of *the Spirit within*. Or we can simply glean from the New Testament Scripture they provided and explain it much easier. Either way, it's all about Christ *in* us. The Old Testament was weighted in God's judgment and punishment for sin and His favor on a natural race of people. The New Covenant is weighted in *the blood*, which makes

connecting to God's goodness and love possible for everyone who believes. The *agape* love of God inside people didn't even exist under the Old—not until Jesus came. That changes everything. God hasn't changed, but the way He deals with people certainly has. If we don't emphasize the New, people are left to drift back toward the darkness that the Old Testament was veiled in. Keep them in the Light.

6. **Follow the Apostle Paul** as he followed Christ. Next to Jesus, Paul is both the best Christian example and also the best Minister example we have. The Lord Jesus used Paul to reveal New Covenant revelation and purpose for the Church, and if we want to succeed, we need to pay close attention to what Paul believed, how he lived, what he emphasized, and what he didn't, "you have carefully followed my doctrine (New Testament), manner of life, purpose (Acts 26:17-18), faith, longsuffering, love, perseverance" (2 Timothy 3:10).

The Holy Spirit— Your Best Friend

1. **Get very familiar with and stay close to your Best Friend.** His name is *Holy Spirit*. He is the person of God, and He is our Guide in life and Ministry. We need fellowship time with Him. We need training time with Him. And we must get familiar with His voice, His unction, and His nature on the inside of us. Jesus spent forty days getting acquainted with the Spirit after being filled. Then "He returned in

the *power of the Spirit* to Galilee" (Luke 4:14). The Spirit is our Leader.

2. **Get familiar with the power**. The Holy Spirit will train you in the power of God if you seek Him about it. We need faith in the power—to be confident that when we need power, it's there, "...that your faith should not be in the wisdom of men but in the power of God" (1 Corinthians 2:5).

3. **When you get out there all alone in Ministry** (and realize that Ministry is absolutely quite lonely), it's just you and Him. If you need comfort, it will be Him who gives it. If you need direction, it comes from Him. If you need power and strength, Holy Spirit is the giver. He must be your best friend. You must love Him the most, "For in him we live, and move, and have our being...For we are also his offspring" (Acts 17:28).

Prayer and Fasting

1. **Ministers must have a healthy prayer life**. To be an excellent Minister, it requires a close connection to the Spirit. To have any power, time with God is essential. Prayer paves the way for all ministry. Without praying, we're basically saying to God, "We can do this ourselves." Stay excellent in your devoted, personal prayer time.

2. **Pray in tongues a lot**. Your ministry depends on it, for that is where we "speak mysteries" and allow the Spirit to give us utterance for the perfect will of God (Romans 8:26-27). Jude 20 says that praying in the

Spirit builds us up on our most holy faith and keeps us in the love of God. At every step of your ministry journey, use your faith to pray it all the way through until you tap into the grace you need. As a Minister, you've got lots of spiritual work to accomplish. Accomplish it first *in the Spirit* by praying in tongues, and then it will succeed.

> The greatest things that ever happened to me…the greatest miracles…the greatest healing miracles…the greatest financial miracles…came after a prolonged time of praying in other tongues. The ministry today…what we're in…what we are doing…what we have been doing for the last number of years…came as a result of praying in other tongues.
>
> —Kenneth Hagin

3. **Fasting is part of every Minister's life**. Especially during preparation for and early in ministry, frequent fasting is necessary to reach a certain level of spiritual maturity and sensitivity to the Spirit. Afterwards, maybe less frequent but occasional fasting is required to maintain that sensitivity. Extended periods of fasting are not mandated, but one to three days here and there can keep you where you need to be. Fasting is not to move God. Fasting is to put your flesh under so your spirit can gain the ascendency and get clarity and faith in your heart.

Apprenticeship

1. **"Men who have a real call are not afraid of apprenticeships"** (Lake, p. 101). Being someone's apprentice, serving faithfully while learning, and committing to another man's vision is imperative for mature development and right perspective. Your time as an apprentice will help you skip the errors that others have made. It will give you time to learn what to do and what not to do. It will carve out your pride and arrogance as you don't get your own way. It will give you the proving ground for true submission and honoring those above you in the Lord so that you can one day reap what you've sown. (And it will provide strength to the man or woman of God you are serving.)

2. **Be faithful in another man's**, "And if ye have not been faithful in that which is another man's, who shall give you that which is your own? (Luke 16:12). It takes courage to build up another person's ministry without continually looking over the fence for your own. Fully commit to someone else and don't be self-seeking or self-promoting. Part of faithfulness is loyalty. And loyalty causes a person to protect the other and never diminish. For example, never publically verbalize opposition to the one you are serving with subtle statements like, "Well, I don't believe it quite like the Pastor...", or "I disagree with that policy". If you disagree, keep it between yourself and the one you are serving. Anything else is out of order.

3. **Patience**—distinguish future glimpses of possibility from your current reality. Realize that the "bigger

thing" you have in heart can come later, but not until you've been excellent in your current assignments.

> Weeds grow quickly, but it takes time for flowers to bloom.
> —Lester Sumrall

Being Number Two, Three, or Four

Some apprenticeships are for a lifetime. And if that is the will of God, it should be enough. Everyone doesn't need their own thing. They don't need their own ministry name, their own non-profit organization, nor their own notoriety. There must always be the number two, three, or four person. Not everyone is called to be the top Minister. Recognize that a *team* of quality Ministers is needed in order for all great works to flourish. This is one of the weaknesses in America, where the entrepreneurial and independent spirit is great on one hand, but not so great in that everyone wants their own thing. Few seem to be content just being *faithful in another man's*.

Full Speed

> Dear ones, do be earnest. Put your whole soul into the work, or else give up.
> —Charles Spurgeon

1. **Ministers are highly self-motivated and compelled**—Ministers should have a continual, burning force in them for the gospel. If it is full enough, then even before an official call, the person will be doing it. Until you are going "seventy miles an hour" in ministering to people, you are not ready for full time Ministry vocation. If you're called, you're driven.

   If you're an Evangelist, you're already going full speed at people, awakening the world and the Church whether there's a pulpit or not. If you are a Pastor, you are already ministering to everyone you run into, finding sheep that you can instruct and help along their journey. If you're a Teacher, your studying has already turned into teaching notes upon notes, and you're already sharing them somewhere somehow. If an Apostle, you're already involved in church planting and gospel foundation building in people. Prophets are not waiting around to prophesy to someone, but are already helping spread the gospel and disciple people. Waiting around to be hand-picked and titled by someone before really getting moving is not how it works. Stay in order and under submission, but get moving.

2. **The nature of a true gift is that it must be given.** So, if we really have something spiritual for the Church, then we're obligated to give it. Don't make the mistake of thinking that God has given the gift *to* you. The gift is for *others*. Actually, *you are* the gift ("and He gave *gifts* to men...Apostles, Prophets..."). That's why Paul could say, "...necessity is laid upon me; yes, woe unto me if I do not preach the gospel" (1 Corinthians 9:16).

Understand what this scripture means, "A man's gift makes room for him, And brings him before great men" (Proverbs 18:16). It doesn't refer to sitting around waiting for others to recognize how great your gift is. It refers to the ancient tradition of going to see a king or a great person—to gain entrance, people would bring a gift and because of the gift, they would be given room to enter and gain audience. For Ministers, you must put faith effort into taking your gift to people.

3. **Open doors are not automatic.** And no one is called to make a way *for you*—it's up to you, your faithfulness, your God, and His grace toward you. God may get people involved with you, but you will need to use your faith to get doors open. Know the anointing and grace that you have, and believe in it enough to take it to people. Use your faith to hear from God, know the will of God, and step out in faith to do the will of God. Get God's strategy, ask God to bring it to pass, confess scriptures to keep yourself confident, and thank God for the open doors. The Lord will open doors no man can shut, but they don't open just by His sovereignty. They open because you use your faith. Remember Jericho? It was totally shut and walled, and God wouldn't open it until Israel heard from God, believed, obeyed, marched, and shouted. Never forget that.

4. **No aggressively pressuring others.** And no pressuring yourself. It is the Lord who actually opens the door, so your job is to keep your trust in Him as you take faith steps.

5. **Don't get the cart before the horse.** Don't be so quick to start a ministry and get your own 501(c)(3) status. Keep the motive focused on the benefit you're supplying to others, and the formal ministry organization can come once it's necessary. Or, maybe your place is in someone else's ministry or in conjunction with a church. Stepping out and going through doors does not mean you have to leave where you are. You can step out and go full speed while staying at a church or under someone else. Use your faith to get things done in partnership unless the Lord has truly launched you out alone. Go full speed, providing a ministry solution to people, rather than focusing on starting the business side of ministry.

Ministry Excellence

1. **God needs quality Ministers.** Commit to it. "And whatever you do in word or deed, do all in the name of the Lord Jesus, giving thanks to God the Father through Him" (Colossians 3:17). There is an old term once used in ministries and churches called "good enough for gospel." That is quite derogatory if you think about it, as if the gospel is a lower calling than worldly ones and doesn't need our best effort at times. But Ministers must keep a high standard for themselves and their ministry activities.

2. **Excellence of heart and character**—excellence begins on the inside of us. Whatever is not great in us needs to be purged. Be conformed to His image. We cannot be *ministry oriented* before being *Son*

oriented. Christianity is about emanating Christ like qualities. Get that right. Get everything right. Put your best effort into yielding to the Holy Spirit so He can make you Kingdom-functional—bold, different, supernatural, loving, fearless, and God-conscious rather than self-conscious. Ministers can't be rough, lazy, weak, or confused in life. They can't be mentally bogged down nor full of trouble in their personal lives. It is not wise to be a Minister who carries around a bag of *emotional hurts*, because hurt people hurt others.

> But in a great house there are not only vessels of gold and silver, but also of wood and clay, some for honor and some for dishonor. Therefore if anyone cleanses himself from the latter, he will be a vessel for honor, sanctified and useful for the Master, prepared for every good work (2 Timothy 2:19-21).

3. **Recognize and bind the strong man.** Whatever the primary area of temptation or struggle is that the devil hounds you over must be eliminated, or you won't reach your full potential in the anointing. And you won't be as effective in helping others. "No one can enter a strong man's house and plunder his goods, unless he first binds the strong man. And then he will plunder his house" (Mark 3:27). So, attack the stronghold in your life and don't stop until your faith gains you the victory.

4. **Always keep your word.** If your word is flimsy, your life and ministry are flimsy. Kenneth E. Hagin said that the mark of a *spiritual pilgrim* is, "He who swears to his own hurt and does not change" (Psalm 15:4).

That means that even if you regret committing to something, do it anyway.

5. **Always be genuine and authentic.** The trust factor is essential in Ministry. Cut out any fakeness from your personality in both the pulpit and also in your relationships. Be willing to acknowledge even cultural or traditional religion in you that really is not *gospel pure*. Be transparent. Be yourself. Or more precisely, be your *new self* in Him, and let your old self "sleep" along with your insecurities. (Transparency and insecurities don't go well together, so get free from *yourself*. There's no greater freedom than *that*.) Don't carry around your secret agenda, trying to control what others do for the benefit of your own welfare, or you'll ruin your relationships. People can detect a game player, and game players lose in life because they can't be trusted (Mark Barclay).

6. **Leading with excellence**—the basis of leadership is the exercise of influence. The basis of influence is the ability to connect with people. To connect with people, you've got to care about them, and you've got to always be honest with them. *Love the people you lead, or you won't be leading anyone for long.* John Maxwell said, "He that thinketh he leadeth, and hath no one following, is only taking a walk."

7. **Excellence is not an act, but a habit.** Weave quality and diligence into everything you do. Your social media sites, web site, business cards, flyers, memos, books, emails, internet posts, and everything else should have excellence in them. Don't be lazy. Use proper grammar, proof your work, get a second opinion, spend some money, and hire someone

when necessary. Ministers represent the Kingdom of God, so everything should be done with quality. God doesn't expect you to feel pressured or go overboard, but He does want you to "prove things that are excellent" (Romans 2:18).

8. **Protect the anointing.** God has entrusted you with a special endowment of the Spirit, and it's your responsibility to keep it paramount in your life. That means to guard against the "little foxes" that could spoil the vine (Song of Solomon 2:15), avoiding choices, circumstances, and neglects that could interfere with the anointing on your life, and avoiding associations with people that despise or belittle the Office.

9. **Start meetings on time,** even if some people haven't arrived. Eventually, most people will sense the need to respect others by being on time.

10. **Pursue excellence, but don't confuse excellence with "perfection".** Don't wait for perfection. You may need to jump out and do things before things seem ready and "perfect", "If you wait for perfect conditions, you will never get anything done" (Ecclesiastes 11:4, NLT). Nothing is ever perfect. But you must do the best you can with the time, ability, and resources that you have.

Vision

1. **Realistic vision**—the lack of it is why Ministers sometimes can't get anywhere (Habakkuk 2:2-3). Whereas *mission* is the motivating purpose behind

what we do, *vision* is more the plan and strategy of how to accomplish the mission. Mission is *doing*, while vision is *being*. Vision is the compilation of your inherent abilities, desires, and execution plan for success. For Ministers, our mission is the same—reach everyone with the gospel, and teach and edify everyone who believes. (That should be clear by now in this handbook.) But vision is more specific—how do *you* plan to get it done? At each phase of your ministry, you will need to know who you are and how you will accomplish the will of God.

2. **Vision begins today.** It is not some big thing that occurs out in the future. Rather, a good vision always includes a place for you now. Certainly, you may have dreams for the future, but with *who you are* right now, what can you do *today*? Are you being faithful with the gift now? Are you preparing diligently? Are you trusting God for opportunities and practicing here and there? For someone who feels to teach or preach, have you offered to teach a class or share a brief Word? Don't let your vision dangle out for when you finally leave your current place, expecting it all to just come to pass once you're out from under the supposed "barrier". Rather, let your gift and vision be examined by your mentors and your peers. If you're finding a vision hard to see or execute, it's possible that you're not really called to the thing in your dream.

3. **Vision for leadership**—for Ministers with their own church or ministry, are you prepared to lead people? You will need to consider all the things necessary for being the "President" of an

organization, including a plan for all operations and a plan to develop and appoint leaders. People will be counting on you, so be sure that your heart has an "eagle" perspective and can see yourself leading people with great wisdom.

4. **Vision to grow the Church**—always have your expectancy alive for church growth and Kingdom growth. It's not about *your* ministry growing, because it's not about the Minister. It's about how you can influence more people toward God. Every Pastor should keep his faith sharp for church growth. God will give you people, servers, and leaders as you do things well and trust him, "Since you were precious in My sight, You have been honored, And I have loved you; Therefore I will give men for you, And people for your life" (Isaiah 43:4). Every traveling Minister should do the same— expect that every place you preach grows. If believers aren't being added to the Church consistently and growing spiritually healthy, you've got to re-examine your vision. If your vision is right, the provision will come.

Sermon and Meeting Preparation

1. **Stay full**. Preaching and teaching is always better when it comes from the overflow of your heart. What your heart knows and meditates on is what you'll end up majoring on, so be sure to know a lot and know it well. If not, you'll seem a bit shallow.

2. **Prepare like there is *no* Holy Spirit. Preach as if there is *only* the Holy Spirit.** Use your faith to prepare well. Then use your faith to trust the Spirit for the words and ministry.

3. **Everyone's preparation will differ.** Some may try and prepare every word ahead of time, while others will prepare very little ahead of time. Some will desire to prepare all week for the message. Others will rather not. Find how God works with you and follow that.

4. **Message style**—the message preached or taught can be evangelistic (with a purpose directed toward final culmination of converting people), exhorting (motivating toward action), topical (choosing a single topic of focus), expository (explaining the meaning of a passage of Scripture, including verse by verse exposition), problem solving (asking and answering a question, such as "Why do prayers go unanswered?"), teaching series (exhausting a topic), or narrative (story-telling of or around a passage). And certainly, many sermons may end up a combination of two or more styles.

5. **If you use notes**, plant them in your heart and get very familiar with them before you teach and preach. You don't want to get lost while you're ministering. So, always double check all Scripture references that you put in your notes during prep time so that *2nd Timothy's* don't become *1st Timothy's* by accident. And be sure to minister not just from planned notes, but preach from the overflow of your heart, and let the Spirit blow on it and take you where He wishes, "If anyone speaks, let him speak as the oracles of God. If anyone ministers, let him do it as with the

ability which God supplies, that in all things God may be glorified through Jesus Christ" (1Peter 4:11).

6. **Diligent to prove things out**—if you hear or read a certain revelation from someone else that seems new or powerful to you, never just take the person's word for it. Study it for yourself. Look up confirming scriptures. Even if it's just a definition or translation of a word that seems to make so much sense, go study it for yourself before you preach it. If you can't confirm certain things that you've heard, either hold off on saying them, or give a disclaimer as you do.

7. **Make a reminder in your notes to avoid common speaking "gap fillers"** like *amen?, right?, um, hallelujah*, etc. while speaking. It will make your preaching better. A silent pause is not a bad thing.

8. **Always pray in the Spirit ahead of time**. Tap in. Look forward, and pour your heart out for the meeting to come. Some say that we should pray in the Spirit at least double the amount of time we're planning on preaching. Maybe so. I wouldn't demand any particular amount, but some substantial time praying in tongues will take your preaching from a C to an A.

By praying in tongues ahead of time, we "connect" our tongue to our spirit man. So, when the teaching or preaching begins, our tongue can easily follow the Spirit as He guides us through the words from Heaven. Also, we're able to pray out things in the Spirit that we're not even aware of. It could be for the specific needs of a person attending. It could be to thwart a plan of the enemy ahead of time. Or, it could be just to prepare yourself. Smith

Wigglesworth said that he had found where "He who speaks in a tongue edifies himself" (1 Corinthians 14:4). So, he said that he would get up and *edify himself* for about an hour and a half, and then go out that night and *edify the people*. So put your faith in the "art" of praying in tongues before meetings (not necessarily the immediate moments prior, but with the meeting in mind).

9. **Look to the Lord ahead of time about the service**. Give Him a chance to show you things to come, what to preach, how to minister, or what you can expect. You won't always receive a specific something from Him, but you've made room for it.

10. **Make room for the Holy Spirit**. Use your faith to follow the flow of the Spirit in meetings rather than your planned agenda. It's okay to have a plan, but you need faith to know when to toss the plan. It is the will of God that determines who operates in which gifts and when manifestations will be given, as it is the "Spirit who works all these things, distributing to each one individually as He wills" (1 Corinthians 12:11). So, we can't just have them every service. But when the Spirit is willing, it is we who must step out for Him to use.

11. **Miracles happen by faith and boldness**—not because we had the whole church spend seven days fasting and praying. Miracles don't happen because God just accidentally decided one day to blow in through the front door. Rather, they happen because someone pulls God's power onto the scene with unwavering expectation. The power of God doesn't come because we sing the perfect mix of songs for the perfect amount of time. It comes

because someone believes God and uses His Name with authority. So make sure your faith is ready to act.

12. **In meetings, be prepared to make a move based on an unction.** God doesn't show us every detail. He requires us to take one step at a time, by faith. Sometimes, all we feel is a certain desire to go minister to someone, knowing nothing of what to say or how to begin. But as we get close, the Spirit begins His work.

Associations and Impartations

1. **Divine connections**—expect that God will assign you and connect you to the right ministers during every phase of ministry. Know who God wants you associated with, and be faithful to it. Ministers need one another. Iron sharpens iron. Make yourself available to others. No Minister should be a "lone ranger", or they will struggle. Ministers should look to be part of a Ministers fellowship, convention, or group of solid Minister friends, however large or small. Just like Peter and John after they were arrested and released, every Minister needs his own "company" to turn to for support, sharpening, and refreshing. Be sure to surround yourself with some successful Ministers, those who've already been there or at least headed where you want to go. Sow into other Ministers' lives, both upward, downward, and at your level.

2. **Ministers need impartation from other Ministers.** God has planned divine associations for us all, not only on the level of receiving teaching, but also on a parent level, "For though you might have ten thousand instructors in Christ, yet you do not have many fathers; for in Christ Jesus I have begotten you through the gospel" (1 Corinthians 4:15). Recognize the opportunities given by the Lord to associate with the right men and women of God and at the right times. Through these associations, impartations happen that are vital to fulfill your call and progress in your ministry. There is something supernatural and endearing that a Minister receives by opening up for someone at the mentor level to speak into his or her life. And this goes the other way as well—look for those whom God entrusts you with mentoring and imparting into.

3. **Be submitted to your peers and to your fathers in the faith.** Paul the Apostle was humble enough to run his preaching and revelation by the other Apostles, just to make sure he hadn't "run in vain" (Galatians 2:1-2). Ministers should keep themselves accountable to others. And since every Minister is also a "sheep", every Minister needs a Pastor.

4. **Ministers must be fed like any other sheep.** Find meetings you can be in to receive a healthy supply of the Word and gospel ministry—*real* meetings (not just online viewing)—a place where your supply of the Spirit and openness allows God to minister to you. No matter how long you've been in ministry, you still need to be in meetings where you are not

doing the preaching. And you need a continual supply of teaching materials and resources.

5. **Eat the fish, but spit out the bones**—recognize that in following some Preachers, you can sometimes follow their faith but not necessarily their doctrine. Just because they have miracles or a big ministry doesn't mean their doctrine is sound in every area.

6. **Pastors will find it difficult and strange to be close friends with church members,** as it's difficult to keep the *shepherd–sheep* relationship clear. The separation to the Office that Ministers go through adds a complexity to relationships. There are exceptions, but church members who get too familiar with their Pastors usually find it harder to esteem and receive from the Office. So, Ministers must have personal friend relationships outside the local assembly and friendships among peers.

Never Forget the Main Thing

1. **Becoming a Minister does not mean we skip being a Christian** or doing what Christians do. The call of the Minister does not replace nor discredit the basic call of every Christian. The first thing Jesus says to every disciple is, "I'll make you fishers of men." It's the real command of Jesus Christ and the first purpose of the Holy Spirit and power—*to be witnesses*. Real Ministers never "graduate" from turning individuals to God. Jesus didn't.

2. **You never take the witness out of the Christian**. The Holy Spirit turns us into witnesses, and that never

changes. Some have thought, *But I'm a Prophet. I have other gifts and things to do.* So was Jesus. He was the greatest Prophet of all, and yet He was a soulwinner. Others think, *But I'm a Pastor with great responsibilities.* So was Jesus. He was and is the Great Shepherd. And yet He wasn't too busy for the woman at the well or the man in the tree. *But I'm an Evangelist and I'm called to big crowds.* So was Jesus. But He shared the gospel everywhere he went, even if it was to only one or a few. You get the picture. Jesus kept the main thing the main thing whether it was in a formal gospel setting or a casual one. And He said, "Follow Me, and I will make *you* [do the same]."

3. **The main thing is not that a *select few Ministers* are to win all the souls**. It is that *Christians* are to do it in their daily lives. Ministers must first be *personal witnesses*, and second, *equippers* of witnesses. Ministers have a daily responsibility to the lost like everyone else. And Ministers equip others for the same. How can a Minister make a well rounded disciple without knowing and doing the main thing himself?

4. **Preachers are given to affect the *saved*, so that the saved can better affect the *unsaved*.** The real reason behind our teaching, our faith building, and our ministering is not to get Christians to vote right in November. It is to make them bright lights to a dark world. The main thing is getting the gospel into the hearts of men, and everyone is to do it.

5. **If the Preachers ignore the Great Commission in their daily lives, the Church will too.**

> Every Christian is either a missionary or an imposter.

—Charles Spurgeon

> If you preachers would start winning souls every-where you go, you wouldn't have to get a book of illustrations to preach from next Sunday.
> —Jack Hyles

> We ought to regard the Christian Church, not a luxurious hostelry where Christian gentlemen may each one dwell at his ease in his own inn, but as barracks in which soldiers are drilled and trained for war.
> —Charles Spurgeon

Beware of Major Pitfalls

God loves His family and wants His Ministers to build it—not harm it. A Minister's fall is harmful not only to their family and friends, but also to the local church, to Christians everywhere, to God, to those who have gone before us, and even to the unsaved world that is watching us, so beware of these pitfalls.

1. **Money**—always do money right. Never get greedy or dishonest. Never do gospel ministry for the money but for God and for people.
2. **Sex and immorality**—be alert and resilient about sex and moral issues. Never compromise your integrity. And never get yourself into compromising situations that have a questionable appearance. People sometimes mistake the appeal of spiritual maturity with a wrong attraction toward Ministers,

so recognize that, and never lead anyone on with endearment or extra attention.

3. **Pride and power**—it is He who deserves the honor for who you are and what you do. So, stay humble before God and people. Be honest and alert to detect where your pride reveals itself, for God resists the proud but gives grace to the humble (James 4:6). Don't get tantalized by power and authority, and don't let your position result in a conceited attitude, treating people roughly and thinking you can act like the high and mighty of the world.

4. **Wrong doctrine**—a Minister is responsible to keep the leaven of false teaching out of the gospel. And beware, as it's usually not everything that's wrong. It can be ninety percent accurate doctrine and ten percent wrong. But just like a little rat poison in food—a little bit can be deadly.

5. **Jumping onto a "cause", especially society-related**—*causes* always lead to distraction and usually—corruption. Even well intentioned "hobbies" can sneak into the pulpit and distract people from Kingdom living and Kingdom building, which should be focused on imparting Spirit filled life into people and not on stopping the vices of society or on world political battles.

6. **Family issues**—be aware that family issues can be a tactic of the devil to throw you off course. He will attempt to use family members and challenges to detour a Preacher with difficulty and strain. Don't let it happen.

7. **Leaders plateau**—don't get complacent in action or in spiritual life. Keep pressing onward and upward—ever progressing.
8. **No balance in life**—the Ministry never stops, and neither does the Minister. However, every Minister must find a way to keep adequate rest in his or her routine and time off for reasonable recreation and leisure. Whatever it takes, the Minister must build habits into his or her life in order to stay in perfect peace. If you're not healthy, spiritually or physically, or if you're overworked without any social balance, it's difficult to help others.

Ordination

To be recognized in a formal Ministry Office, ordination is the proper process. Technically, the Lord is the one who sets a person in Office, so He is the initial ordainer, "Ye have not chosen me, but I have chosen you, and ordained you, that ye should go and bring forth fruit" (John 15:16). But subsequently, we should continue with appropriate Church doctrine and formal ordination, so as to be in order with those who have gone before us and for the sake of the Church. Paul told Titus, "...set in order the things that are lacking, and appoint (ordain) elders in every city as I commanded you" (Titus 1:5). There are certainly exceptions where people end up in Ministry before any official ordination ceremony or laying on of hands, but it is still a doctrine.

Commonly, the first step within most organizations or churches is to be *licensed*, which is obviously not a Scriptural term but rather a way for a church or ministry to acknowledge a believer who wishes to begin the proving stage of their call, giving them accepted credentials for recognition inside and outside the organization. After ample time giving evidence to a legitimate call of God (usually between six months and two years), the person is eligible for *ordination*. In many states, both licensing and ordination carry the same secular rights of a Minister being a representative of the state for marriages (learn the rules of your state). But from the Church perspective, the important thing is the spiritual approval of those above the Minister for his or her public acknowledgement.

Missionaries

Here is a brief list of special considerations for missionaries.

1. **A *need* is not a *call*.** Just because you are burdened for orphans in Africa doesn't mean you're called as a missionary there. Just because you have compassion for prisoners doesn't mean you're to be in prison ministry. You must follow the Spirit into God's will.

2. **When traveling overseas to minister, be prepared for cultural differences.** Most third world countries still have rampant bribery as a form of business, which usually begins at the airport. Investigate ahead of time the things to avoid, such as terminology, body movements, humor, etc. For example, in some countries, it's offensive to whistle. In some countries, they bow rather than handshake.

And in most places, your type of humor may not go over so big, so avoid most of it. There are differences in clothing requirements (especially women), interaction among genders, family practices, nursing babies in public and in church, etc. Be prepared.

3. **When preaching with a translator**, trust God and possibly make the request for one who is also a Preacher themselves in order to minimize how much is lost in the translation.

4. **Eat what they give you** (unless there is possible contamination from parasites or things washed in local water and not fully cooked). Sleep where they put you. But don't be afraid to make requests when necessary. And only drink bottled water unless you know for certain the local water is safe. In many places, it's not contaminated water that's the problem, but rather the high natural mineral content that we're not accustomed to. Use the internet to research things ahead of time.

5. **Only go when it's the will of God**. And be sure your faith in God is strong for divine protection, divine provision, divine health, and divine guidance. And then don't be afraid of anything.

Chapter 6
Money

Some folks don't like the mention of money along with the gospel, as there's been quite the conflict and abuse through the years. But that's nothing new. Even Paul mentioned that Ministers shouldn't be "greedy for filthy lucre". However, that does not displace the principle that "...the Lord has commanded that those who preach the gospel should live from the gospel" (1 Corinthians 9:14), and "He has pleasure in the prosperity of His servant" (Psalm 35:27). It is God's plan that Ministers should be paid for their gospel work—enough to fully live on. But a Minister must take the responsibility to do money right in every way before God and man so as not to bring reproach on the Body of Christ, and also to fully complete his or her assignment.

1. **God is your source**—not the people, not the church offerings, not special meetings, not your mailing list, and not products. Don't ever look at the people, not their faces, not their clothes or lifestyle, and not the number of them. Don't ever pressure anybody to give you anything in the Name of God or gospel. Leave them alone about money.

Only look at God as your Provider. Know His promises. Build your faith in His Word about money. Focus your attention on Matthew 6, God's basic Finance 101 class for the Christian, until you are secure in your faith and free from the pursuit of money. Until you learn to trust God and believe Him alone for your finances, you will struggle in the Ministry.

Avoid slipping into the mental arena of trying to find how to make money from the gospel. If you truly work for God, He will pay.

2. **No manipulation**—no hinting to people about your financial situation or your favorite car. No buddying up to wealthy people with an ulterior motive. No examining the offerings too closely and being a respecter of persons. No looking for "preacher's discounts" everywhere you go. No prophesying money out of people's pockets. Go the other direction like Paul did so as not to be accused of being a burden on others or of using his office deceitfully (2 Thessalonians 3:7-8). If you get under real financial strain, of course you can get advice or prayer from your confidants, but keep the motive pure. "For neither at any time did we use flattering words, as you know, nor a cloak for covetousness, God is witness" (1 Thessalonians 2:5).

3. **You have to *work*.** Great Ministers are great workers. If you will spend forty to fifty hours a week teaching, preaching, going after people, ministering to people, and building the Kingdom, God will pay you a forty to fifty hour a week salary somehow. And if you spend the rest of your time preparing yourself

and developing yourself in the Spirit, God will promote you. If you're not making it financially, get a secular job and supplement your income, doing whatever is necessary. Do it with faith and without condemnation, and trust God for the grace that you need. If the financial difficulty is perpetual even after you've endured for a long while, something may be wrong—either your faith in God needs improvement, or your timing was wrong, or something else, because in God's will, His supply is always sufficient (2 Corinthians 9:8).

4. **For new endeavors, vision comes before *pro*-vision.** First you need a project plan and reason, and then you need to put action toward it, or you'll never see the supply. Waiting for money before venturing out to do something is like the children of Israel crying at the edge of the Red Sea. God told Moses to stop crying and do something about it—to stretch forth his rod (of authority) and tell the children of Israel to start walking across. Like Elisha's solution for the armies of Israel and Judah that had no water, "Make this valley full of ditches"—after they put in the faith effort and gave God a place to put the blessing, God did His supernatural thing and filled the ditches with water. You've got to give God the faith project before He can supply for it.

If you sense the will of God to do something, don't look at the bank account to see if it can be done. Believe God and start heading forward so your faith can come alive. Then God will supply. If you need a project done, use your faith. If you need an employee, hire one by faith. Timing may be important, but at some point, you'll need to take a step of faith before you see any supply.

5. **Teach your people to give generously.** Neither the Pastor nor the people should have a poverty mentality for funding a church or ministry. You must teach your people to give tithes and offerings not only to build the church, the kingdom, and provide for the Ministers, but also because they love God and trust Him. Tithing is trusting. Regardless of how much a person earns or has, their heart will never be fully in at a church until they can give a legitimate portion of tithes and offerings, "For where your treasure is, there your heart will be also" (Matthew 6:21). If their treasure is not in their church, neither is their heart.

   No one should be in it for the money. But it doesn't mean that a church or ministry should be living on hand-me-downs. Successful ministry requires money. So don't be a cheapskate when it comes to fully funding the ministry. The Minister and leaders should get their faith built up to receive the necessary funds in a proper manner. Bake sales and barely-usable donations are not the way to pay for ministry needs. Teach the people that generosity includes *firstfruits* giving, which is the first and best portion rather than the leftovers. People need to be taught to value the Kingdom to the point that if a need arises, someone just steps up with an offering rather than a new scheme to sell trinkets or chicken plates.

6. **No poverty mentality for paying Ministers**—Ministers should not have to scrape crumbs to get

by. Ministers once were encouraged to take a "vow of poverty" when entering the Ministry. But that is unscriptural. Certainly, we should be willing to remain in Ministry no matter the circumstance. But in no way does the Bible say Ministers can't benefit and be provided for. It says just the opposite. So, keep an excellent mindset of *compensation for the value of services rendered*. Of course, don't go overboard or get lustful about money, but do things well.

7. **Pay yourself.** In the Ministry, it feels like we should use all the income for more ministry. But be wise. God would never muzzle the ox that treads the corn (1 Corinthians 9:9), and He would never expect a Preacher to muzzle himself. Certainly, volunteering is a huge part of Church life and ministry roles, and Preachers usually end up doing plenty of "pro-bono" work. But if you're the one cutting checks, be sure to cut yourself one. If you don't, then who will? If we truly value gospel ministry, we should feel right about compensating ourselves (and others when appropriate) for it. "Let the elders who rule well be counted worthy of double honor, especially those who labor in the word and doctrine" (1 Timothy 5:17).

8. **Plan and fund your future.** Though Ministers never "retire", it only makes sense to have a solid nest egg planned for our final twenty years or so. In the past, it became popular among Christians to neglect saving any money and get rid of retirement accounts since Jesus was coming soon. He is coming soon, but *soon* is relative. Follow the Bible principle of "he who gathers little by little shall be increased", and save

money each month after you've given to God. Pay God first. Pay yourself second (savings). Pay your bills last. Set up a 403(b) or IRA and begin funding it monthly.

9. **Social Security and wisdom**—in the U.S., Ministers are allowed to opt out of paying Social Security tax. But if you do that, know that you're also opting out of *receiving* Social Security *income* later (aside from what you've already paid in if you're fully vested). That means that you don't get to *spend* your extra cash, but that you *save and invest* it somewhere else. If you don't, you're not being excellent or wise. If you're going to opt out of Social Security, you better be a faith person and have a plan.

10. **Think about your employees' future.** Use your faith to pay them well, and teach them to add *their* monthly faith to yours, so everyone is paid. If you are the boss, you are responsible to make something available for them. Consider setting up a 403(b) for their last two decades of life and possibly even matching a percentage of their contributions, just like any company might do for its employees. (Include yourself in that, too, as you're an employee).

11. **Tithing and giving to your local church doesn't stop because you're a Minister.** You shouldn't *tithe* to yourself, even though you're in the Ministry. That's not how it works. (Don't make the mistake of trying to tie the Old Testament tithe and priesthood to the Church today. *Preachers* today have not replaced *priests* of the Old Testament. It is different. Priests were *mediators and part of the tribe who had no*

inheritance. We are not. Jesus is our Mediator, and we don't need another.) Giving to God is a principle that keeps us trusting Him and valuing Him with our substance, partly because we are *parting* with something of value. Even if your salary may come from your church or ministry, you are a church member first, so keep doing your part like everyone else. Continue your own personal partnership and giving with other ministries, and also establish partnership through your church or ministry with other ministries. You'll find that the principle of sowing and reaping is essential even to your own church or ministry.

12. **Church and ministry include a business side.** If you want to see your ministry grow, you will need to be excellent with money and keep all records straight and honest. Just as Jesus had an accountant with Him, and just as they had to stay in order with "Caesar", we will need similar order in our ministries. Do all things above board. Never cheat. Stay abreast of all legal and financial requirements, and do it right. And establish office procedures, oversight, and checks and balances for all money matters that you and staff will follow (e.g. always have more than one usher or staff handling the offerings to eliminate suspicion and temptation).

13. **Separate *ministry* from *personal*.** The government wants a clear distinction from what a church or ministry owns versus what a Minister owns personally. Own your own stuff and don't use the church's stuff. Don't let church members borrow church property for personal use. Pastors should

not own the church or the property, but keep it separate. Cars, too, in most cases. If driving a church vehicle, keep good records for personal versus ministry related mileage, and do it right. Don't co-mingle funds by having your church or ministry pay for personal items.

Chapter 7
Our 50+ Ministry Success Tips

1. **Lift up no man but Jesus**, put down no man but the devil, and get your messages from Heaven. Pastors should never get down on and bitter against church members. And other Ministers should never get bitter against Pastors who aren't doing it the way they want. And certainly never speak out loud about it, or you'll get reprimanded by God, "Who are you to judge another's servant? To his own master he stands or falls" (Romans 14:4).
2. **Preach only what you practice**. And preach only what you *know*. You can borrow information, but you can't borrow revelation. For preaching to have the anointing necessary to penetrate hearts, it can't be just a mental transfer of knowledge that you got from someone else. Second hand revelation isn't revelation until you get it into your own heart and prove it out for yourself.
3. **Treat every assignment with the same honor.** Preach to the one or to the few as sincerely as you would to the large crowd. Realize that God and

others over you will give you seemingly insignificant assignments that are actually pivotal tests of your attitude and motives.

4. **Never minister out of your own difficulty.** Wait until you can prove out the solution and the trouble is over before you testify and use it as an example or something. Never expose your current misery, as that never blesses people. Preach on something else. No one wants to follow a leader who is dragging up the rear. "Watch, stand fast in the faith, be brave, be strong" (1Corinthians 16:13). Never let them see you scared. We all have obstacles. But as a leader, do not lift up the obstacles before the people because, it will "melt their hearts" like it did Israel when the ten spies complained about the giants.

5. **Spend your time on, and focus only on those who will listen.** In every congregation, even youth and children, there are those who are open and tuned in, and there are those who are distracted. Even if it's just one out of ten who are interested, focus only on the one, and don't be distracted by the others. If a chaotic one is distracting others, get them out rather than spend your time correcting them and taking away from the open ones. You'll realize that much time can be wasted on the weak ones, the disinterested ones, and the unfaithful ones.

6. **When you look at people, see only their potential and not their shortcomings.** God uses the foolish things to confound the wise, so see an army of able soldiers instead of a disheveled bunch. Not many mighty and noble are called (1 Corinthians 1:26), so develop the weak. King David turned 400

distressed, poor, scared and discontent men into the army of a king. Faith people may start off weak but can end up strong, "out of weakness were made strong" (Hebrews 11:34).

7. **Know what type of service you are having.** Is it a Bible teaching service, a prayer service, or a healing service? Whatever type it is, major on that. Ministers make the mistake sometimes of trying to combine every type of service into one, when the Spirit may be wanting to focus on one particular thing. Not every service needs extended worship and praise time, possibly none or rather just a song or two to kick it off and get people in one accord.

8. **Don't drag meetings on** when the anointing has lifted and they should be over. There is a benefit to being left a bit hungry every week rather than overloaded.

9. **Don't let your church become just a "hospital".** Certainly, part of what we do is bring healing to the sick. But not everyone is sick, and no one wants to feel like they're visiting an infirmary every Sunday morning. So when they hear, "So-n-so's sick. Let's all remember and pray" every service, it drags everyone through the sorrow. So, don't feel obligated to report all the sick people or dead people who are missing from church. This is a ploy of the devil, distracting from the ministry of the Word and putting a "wet blanket" on any atmosphere of faith and rejoicing. Either heal the sick and get it done, or tend to them afterward, but don't bring everyone along "to the hospital bed" during normal church services (*exception* cases are the exception). It's too

discouraging. Sure, we are to care and bear burdens, but let that be done in the smaller group setting or one on one rather than with the entire congregation all the time.

10. **Never be people's Holy Spirit**. Rather, help them hear from God themselves. Never control, dominate, or lord your position over people. Always lead rather than push, pull, or yank. And don't be their "convictor". The Spirit can handle that. Good followers will follow your example.

11. **Don't hold back the Word of God** or personal correction for fear of offending people. Deep down, church members want the Pastor and Preachers to have backbone. (Just like teenagers, who deep down, appreciate parents who have backbone.) Paul said to the elders of Ephesus, "I testify to you this day that I am innocent of the blood of all, for I did not shrink from declaring to you the whole counsel of God" (Acts 20:26-27). Speak the truth in love.

12. **Preach the Word—not your personal lifestyle convictions.** Just because the Lord may be dealing with you on a certain issue, it doesn't mean it's for everyone. Leave your anti-coffee, anti-cheeseburger, "organic only" commands at home with your natural family, and don't bring it to church. Harping on natural things that aren't in Scripture will heap condemnation on people. And it will ruin the gospel atmosphere. (See 1 Timothy 4:3-5 for our New Testament eating principle.)

13. **Rely on the Bible**, and don't lean very heavily on other historical resources for your preaching. Use examples and lessons from history if you wish, but

don't be too adamant about the spiritual legitimacy of your historical "proof". Some historians such as Josephus, or even modern day researchers, write things that may be valid and true, but *only Scripture is infallible*. And if you did accidentally glimpse something from somewhere, the rule of interpretation is always that *nothing from God will ever contradict other things from God*.

14. **The Preacher is not the chef. He's only the server.** God doesn't need you to make up a fancy meal. He only needs you to deliver the meal to the table without messing it up. So, don't try and embellish Scripture. Don't try and make it say what you want it to say. And don't use loose revelation, unless you tell the people that "this might possibly be the case, but I'm not sure". Don't try to guess what something means. And don't say "God told me this scripture means" if you cannot prove it with other scriptures. If you feel you've received some new revelation, be sure to prove it out Scripturally and practically before you preach it. And possibly run it by someone if it's that new. Prophets are commanded to "let the other judge" (1 Corinthians 14:29). So all Ministers should make submission a habit.

15. **Stay genuine in the pulpit**. The gospel is real, so the Minister should be real. Preaching should be colloquial (language that is used in ordinary or familiar conversation; not formal or literary) and should not be a theatrical fabrication. Certainly, any time the Word of God is preached, whether it is done in a great way or weak way, mighty things can happen because the Word is alive and the gospel contains the power. But cut out unnecessary

theatrics that may distract from the message or draw attention to a parading personality. Being animated and expressive and *having* personality is absolutely fine, and that's not being referred to here. What is being said is that preaching doesn't have to be religiously weird or pseudo-stylish to be effective. Charles Finney, one of the great Evangelists of the Second Great Awakening, said,

> I wish to make a few remarks on the manner of preaching. It should be conversational. Preaching, to be understood, should be colloquial in style. A minister must preach just as he would talk, if he wishes fully to be understood. Nothing is more calculated to make a sinner feel that religion is some mysterious thing that he cannot understand than this formal, lofty style of speaking which is so generally employed in the pulpit. The minister ought to do what the lawyer does when he wants to make a jury understand him perfectly. He uses a style perfectly colloquial. This lofty, swelling style will do no good. The gospel will never produce any great effects until ministers talk to their hearers, in the pulpit, as they talk in private conversation (Finney, p. 214).

> The Bishop of London once asked Garrick, the celebrated actor, why it was that actors, in representing a mere fiction, should move an assembly, even to tears, while ministers, in representing the most solemn realities, could scarcely obtain a hearing. The philosophical Garrick well replied: 'It is because we represent fiction as reality, and

you represent reality as fiction' (Finney, p. 228).

Stay genuine. The question to ask yourself is, *Would He who knows your heart be pleased with how you're acting or presenting yourself?*

16. **Never do anything to violate your conscience.** God will uphold you in your integrity (Psalm 41:12). If you don't have integrity, He won't. Get to a place of pure honesty—honest about yourself, honest with God, and honest in all your words and dealings. If you violate your conscience, learn how to "sprinkle or plead the blood of Jesus" over it by faith, get forgiven, and be clean in your heart. And do that until you've cleaned up your act. And teach your people how to do the same, for "sin consciousness is the reason for practically every spiritual failure" (Kenyon, p. 14). People won't serve God fervently if they have a sin consciousness.

17. **Top things the sheep ask of you**: Don't get messed up with sex, don't get messed up with money, and don't be self-indulgent. Be Scriptural, be honest, challenge us to go further, and be an example in every way. Don't be too much like us—be better.

18. **Do money right**. Whatever it takes, get every single trace of dishonesty out of you. Manipulation tactics are rampant in the Church today. Don't fall into using them. Trust only God, and never misuse your office, "Feed the flock of God which is among you, taking the oversight thereof, not by constraint, but willingly; not for filthy lucre, but of a ready mind" (1 Peter 5:2 KJV). No pressuring, no begging, no "we're going broke if you don't give", and no "I'll pray

a special blessing on everyone who gives a $100 bill". And don't ever use the pulpit to sell something for yourself or others—no pyramid schemes. Behind closed doors, no skimming off the offering, no tricks, and no justifying questionable actions. Every offering is holy, so treat it as being entrusted with God's money. He knows exactly what you're thinking, so be perfect about it.

19. **Get familiar with the Spirit of God and His power in you.** You will need to know how He leads you in ministry. And you will need confidence in getting His power on the scene when necessary, "That your faith should not be in the wisdom of men but in the power of God" (1 Corinthians 2:5). One of the responsibilities of a Minister is to be sensitive to the Spirit (Ed Dufresne). No Minister is effective without a lifestyle in the Holy Spirit.

20. **Walk in love. Pray in tongues.** You need the presence of God dripping off you like a sponge. For that to happen, your love walk is paramount. And for your love walk to flourish, you'll need to pray in tongues every day (Jude 20-21). Praying in tongues will keep you sensitive to the Spirit, refreshing to people, and full of joy.

21. **Pastor, minister, and lead by the Spirit.** Pray in tongues a lot and stay in the Spirit so you can see and know things. Deal with things in the Spirit before you address them in the natural. Sometimes, if you'll deal with issues in prayer first, the Lord will solve the problem or make a troublemaker leave before you have to get involved. Other times, you'll need to recognize how not to "uproot the wheat with

the tares". And still other times, you'll need faith and grace to step in and handle something proactively. So stay in the Spirit.

22. **Ministering in the Spirit and power**—never feel pressured to perform, to say something when it's quiet, or to minister in power. Let it flow from the Spirit and from the pull of the people in the Spirit. And never forget that signs accompany *the Word preached* (Mark 16:20). Also, after doing something in the Spirit, do not feel obligated to justify what has happened with a statement like, "we just let the Spirit move here", or "see, if I hadn't been sensitive and obedient, we wouldn't have had that move of the Spirit", or "did you feel the presence of God just now?" If it was God, they felt it and were blessed and happy even if they didn't know the details. And many times, there will be only a few who are touched by God personally. So, just let the ministry run its course rather than pressure and confuse those who did not "feel" it. Then later, on another day, you can use that as a teaching tool and remind people what and why things happened. Of course, we should always thank Him for His blessing after He has blessed.

23. **Faith for miracles, salvations, and growth**—these things require constant expectation and faith toward God from the Minister. Believe that God wants them to happen more than you. And believe that He will bring it to pass based on your request and desire. Results happen because someone believed God, and not because of a large number of people praying. That's why huge prayer chains don't work. Miracles are never an accident. And neither are salvations and

revival. When something happens, it's because someone close to and with rightful authority in the situation prayed with compassion and confidence. Bathe your endeavors in prayer, and believe God. Revival happens because someone cared so deeply and wanted it so badly they couldn't live without it.

24. **Jesus' spiritual motivators should be yours, too.** Hebrews 1:9 unveils the secret behind Jesus' anointing, "You have loved righteousness and hated lawlessness; Therefore God, Your God, has anointed You with the oil of gladness more than Your companions." When you love what is right and hate what is wrong, the anointing in your life will increase. Also, notice the motive behind Jesus healing people. Many times the scriptures say that Jesus was "moved with compassion" when He healed the sick or cast out devils. The anointing in your life will increase to the degree of your compassion for people.

25. **Pastoring is like driving a bus.** People will get on, and people will get off. Don't be concerned about people leaving your church. That's just the nature of "bus driving". Baby lambs bop all around and in and out. Just let them. And sometimes even mature sheep leave. Don't try to hang onto people who have left. This is probably one of the hardest challenges in Ministry, but it happens. And there is a real faith needed to cast the care to God and not let your heart be damaged by feelings of betrayal and dishonor. The reality is that many times those who we thought were with us but left us were never really with us in the first place, "They went out from us,

but they were not of us; for if they had been of us, they would have continued with us; but *they went out* that they might be made manifest, that none of them were of us" (1 John 2:19).

26. **The front door**—Pastors, don't worry about the back door (people leaving church). But, use your faith to *open the front door wider*. Realize that the people who are with you are just a small average percentage of the much larger group that came by and didn't stay with you. So, rather than fret over a low retention percentage, use your faith to enlarge the visiting group so that your church grows in spite of that retention percentage. Trust God that He decides who connects to your ministry, and leave that part to Him. Do church the best you can, and then just put your faith out for more guests to venture in and through.

27. **"Develop one blind eye and one deaf ear if you want to survive Ministry"**—Charles Spurgeon. Ignore most drama and all offense, doing the love walk around it. And teach the people the same. Be emotionally tough-skinned, or you'll taint the people with a sour attitude.

28. **Whatever you're into as a leader, the people will eventually get into**. If you're into prayer, the people will be. If you're a giver, they will give. If you're a Bible reader, they will be too. If you're into personal witnessing, they will catch it. If you're into music, you'll gain a following of the same. If you're into national politics, guess what?

29. **The book of Acts is somewhat our pattern for modern day Kingdom style**. Though the Church is

no longer in infancy stage, and though culture and tradition has changed, what makes the heart glad has not. True spiritual health is the only thing worthwhile, so although strategies differ from ministry to ministry, stay with the fundamentals found in the book of Acts: *Continue in the Apostles doctrine, fellowship, breaking of bread, prayers, and the Word of God. Go find people, and tell the gospel. If they're already disciples, teach them better. If they are powerless, help them receive the Spirit. If you're persecuted, rejoice. Follow the Holy Spirit in your ministry. Expect the miraculous. Expect the angels to help you. Live by faith. Know the grace of God, and don't go back to law. Emphasize tongues and gifts of the Spirit. And keep acting on the Word of God. Contend for the faith and power of the early Church.*

30. **Shepherds keep their sheep healthy enough to bear more sheep.** Shepherds don't bear sheep. Sheep bear sheep. So, keep the Great Commission, the high calling of the Church, before the people. And teach them how to fish for men. Also, understand this very important aspect of making converts: strangers that you or your church members lead to Jesus out in the public will probably never come to your church. It seems like we should have a strict follow-up and disciple process for those who confess Christ, so that they're not left alone after salvation. However, in my twenty years of experience, it is consistent that for a new convert, rather than automatically go to a stranger's church, they will first connect with someone they are familiar with—maybe a Christian family member or friend. So, the person who leads them to Christ must find solace as

Philip did after leading the eunuch to the Lord in Acts 8—the Spirit caught Philip away and he never saw him again. And God didn't mind. There is a principle that Jesus presented—that we would reap where we don't sow and sow where we don't reap (John 4:36-38). Even Paul mentioned how he planted, Apollos watered, but God gave the increase. We have an obligation to lead others to Jesus, regardless of what happens afterward.

31. **Teach people to read their Bibles** *in the Spirit* rather than just with their mind. Teach them to read the Old Testament *in the light of* the New Testament. If you don't remind them of that a lot, they will drift back to a life of condemnation rather than righteousness. And they will develop a feeling of threat and worthlessness rather than grace, goodness, and favor. We obey God now by faith rather than by law. We receive the blessing by faith now rather than strictly by obedience, as the belief in the heart is paramount in this New Covenant. For instance, if a person is perfectly obedient to all ten commandments, but doesn't believe in Jesus Christ, do they have eternal life? No. If a person is perfectly good to his fellow man all the days of his life, but doesn't believe in healing by faith (Mark 5:34), will God miraculously heal him when he asks? No. Faith is the catalyst, "But before faith came, we were kept under guard by the law...Therefore the law was our tutor to bring us to Christ, that we might be justified by faith. But after faith has come, we are no longer under a tutor" (Galatians 3:23-25).

32. **Never forget Luke 10:19**, and never let your people forget Luke 10:19. Nothing can hurt you. And

nothing can hurt them—if you and they can believe it. Luke 10:19 can be life-changing.

33. **Stay with the fundamentals**. The basics were our first love. Even though you may have matured and may be fully adept at the basic doctrines, remember that those basics are the foundation for the next new believers, and new believers are thrilled to hear them taught. Many Ministers have gotten off track by forgetting that. They've gotten carried away with dramatic showmanship, winds of doctrine, and "new teachings" that make for fame and money and bring the ooh's and aah's, and they will answer for it one day. Preach the basics as if no one has heard them.

34. **Don't build "needy" people.** The goal in teaching and preaching is to develop people into disciples of Christ who can stand on their own rather than insinuate that you are their crutch for life. Teach them to trust God for themselves and hear God for themselves so that they're not always running to the altar for prayer or prophecy. Teach them how to pray for others rather than you being the only one who can get power on the scene. Basically, "equip the saints for the work of the ministry" rather than allow them to remain infants in need of milk.

35. **"Lay your hands on the people often."** —Oral Roberts. Laying on of hands is a foundational doctrine of Christ, so don't neglect it (Hebrews 6:2). Laying hands may be done for healing (James 5:14-15), for impartation and ordination (1 Timothy 4:14, 2 Timothy 1:6, Acts 13:3), for the baptism of the Holy Spirit (Acts 8:18, 9:17, 19:6), and for

blessing (Mark 10:16). People need the touch as a point of connection to God.

36. **Counseling**—most of the counsel that people need happens during the main teaching and preaching to the congregation. The better the teaching is, the less counseling you should be doing. Many times, the real problem with the person in need of counseling is that they're not in church regularly. If they would just attend church every week, they would see that all their issues had recently been addressed. When a person shows up for regular church, they give the Spirit the chance to move in their heart and life. So, point that out, and don't always feel obligated to give people special office time when they haven't even shown up for the main meetings. On the occasion that someone does need some counseling time, be led by the Spirit in how much time you give them, where you meet, what advice you give from God's Word, and notice how receptive they are. Be aware that many times, people have already made up their minds regardless of how great your advice is, so don't take it personally. (Note: do not use the word "counseling" or "counselor", as there are legal implications in the U.S. and a formal license is required in most states to be called a "Counselor". Just use the term "meeting" or "instructing".)

37. **Material things are given in response to spiritual things**. Keep the *Preacher—believer* relationship proper by realizing that Preachers give the gospel and minister *spiritual things* to people. And people give *money and material things* to Preachers. "If we have sown spiritual things for you, is it a great thing if we reap your material things?" (1 Corinthians

9:11). You'll find in ministry of any sort, that there will always be opportunity to help someone out financially. And sometimes you may choose to do it. However, you'll also notice that if it's not done as led by the Spirit, it will throw the relationship out of order. As soon as someone gets money rather than spiritual ministry from a Minister, it closes them just a little from being able to receive the spiritual. If repeated, the person will begin to use the Minister as a source for material aid and will close off completely. Then, being out of order, immaturity and offense is usually the next result. Be led by the Spirit. Churches should be able to help the saints who are in need, but primarily only if they are part of that local church, and only if it's done with some sort of vetting and oversight. If possible, delegate the benevolence ministry to someone other than the Ministers, just as the early Church did with the first deacons.

38. **Prosperity is God's covenant promise no matter which country you live in.** So learn it, preach it, and expect it, or the people will never reach their potential in life or in Kingdom-building. Many people think that the United States is synonymous with prosperity, but it's not. God is. Most people in America are worried about money and feel poor just like people in other lands. Prosperity doesn't begin in the United States. It begins on the inside of us. So, it can happen for any Christian in any country at any time they believe in and act on God's covenant in Christ.

39. **Choose your leaders by the Spirit.** Look for those that you can touch *spirit to spirit*. Who are they?

They are the ones you have a spiritual "spark" with. If you can't touch their spirit, something's wrong and they're not with you. Look for those who have your heart and vision and those who are loyal rather than those who just have ability. If it doesn't feel quite right, don't force it or you'll get stuck with people who are in it for themselves, and it may be hard to get them out. Some people may wonder why you're not appointing them since they have skills and such. Don't bother about that. You're simply waiting for the right things. If they ask, you can investigate their heart. But you are not obligated to those who have heart issues until they get it straight.

40. **Be careful of promising people positions**. Notice how when Jesus chose His disciples, He didn't promise they would be leaders of the Church—not at first. At first, He only said, "Follow me". In the gospel, faithfulness must be voluntary without promise and obedient to God without reward. Sometimes it's necessary to hire people with a promise, but keep it few and far between. Anything more borders on *flattery* (1 Thessalonians 2:5). We've found that the most pure service to the Lord is when a person has volunteered from their heart long before receiving any position or payment, and then they might become eligible.

41. **Detect when your leaders have disconnected in their heart**. Sometimes, they're just going through personal things. But it's also possible that a root of bitterness has sprung up in them over an offense concerning you. And if someone has allowed that to happen toward you, subsequent events are sure to follow that are difficult to repair. Though our first

inclination is certainly mercy and love, be aware that if the bitterness is not completely uprooted, eventually others will be affected. So, if someone refuses to mend your relationship, be quick to let that relationship go until they repent.

42. **Church growth plateau**—if you're a Pastor, and your church seems to have become stale, hit a plateau in growth, or is diminishing, it may be because of one of these disconnected leaders. Once you "help" them leave, you'll find an immediate freedom again in church and a quick recovery. It also may be because of some demonic operation against the church. If that is the case, deal with it swiftly and sharply in the Spirit, commanding it to cease and desist. Then be done with it. Don't carry on about it, telling all the church to pray and such. All that does is build people's faith in some huge obstacle against them. If you need a couple of people to help you pray and deal with it, fine. But know your authority and get it done. (Of course, there can be other reasons for church growth to stagnate.)

43. **Out of your heart flows the whole church**. "Keep your heart with all diligence, for out of it *spring* the issues of life" (Proverbs 4:23). As a leader, it is important that only the right things are in your heart, for they will permeate the Church. If you have bitterness, the people will feel it. If you have doubt or discouragement, they will too. If you get sidetracked, it's not only yourself that you will answer for. On the other hand, if you stay fresh, free, and pure in your heart, the people will catch that, too.

44. **Enjoy God above all else!** Remember your first love? Keep your primary delight in your prayer time and fellowship with the Spirit. If you do that, you'll never get bored, mad at life, or hopeless. No matter what's going on in your family or your ministry, your time with God should be your most joyful place.

45. **Don't forget the prophecies and words spoken to you** (1 Timothy 1:18). Remember the pure call you received from the Lord. Embrace it and live out of it. Forget everything in between if you have to.

46. **Focus on the good**. Praise God for any success. And ignore the seeming failures. Focus on who's there—not on who's absent. Focus on the fruit that you do get and not on what you don't. Thankfulness for what you *do* have and for the *good things* is the key to a consistently successful endeavor.

47. **Stay in your lane**. Know your call, know your part and place, and stay with it. Change only if and when God requires. Be the best at who and what you are. And don't know yourself by the flesh but by your identity in Christ and the anointing within.

    Whatever grace you have, be glad about it and don't go looking for a different grace. If you try to push into things you're not called to, the devil will accommodate you and shove you out of God's will. Even great men and women of faith have fallen into this trap, not being satisfied with a wonderful miracle and healing ministry, and trying to be a Teacher instead. Or attempting to do spectacular miracles and give great prophecies instead of just using their great preaching gift. And people will occasionally pressure Ministers to do so with comments like, "Why don't you ever 'xyz' like so-n-so?" Don't fall for it.

48. **Never compare yourself to others.** Everyone is in their own race. Learn to rejoice at others' success and glorify God for the grace upon others' ministries. Another person doing great things doesn't say anything about *you*. If something motivates you or encourages you, fine. But don't feel discouraged by someone who seems ahead of you, or prideful that you may be ahead of someone else. It's all between you and the Lord, and them and the Lord.

> For we dare not class ourselves or compare ourselves with those who commend themselves. But they, measuring themselves by themselves, and comparing themselves among themselves, are not wise (2 Corinthians 10:12).

49. **Don't get bored. Don't lose your fire. And don't become dull hearted,** "For the shepherds have become dull-hearted and have not sought the Lord; therefore they shall not prosper" (Jeremiah 10:21). If you feel yourself losing a bit of faith and zeal, shut down and fast for a day or two. Get back to your Bible and to prayer, and God will meet you quickly. We never outgrow being a Christian, and all Christians must spend time in the Word and prayer for personal strength, or we'll grow cold, weak, and ineffective. Don't let the busyness of ministry take away from your own spiritual health.

Know this—that no matter how spiritually *low* you ever feel and how far from your course you feel that you're on, you're not really all that far. As a matter of fact, it's all still right there beyond "the veil". Sometimes after a little spiritual drought, it feels like it may take months of seeking God to find Him again. But it doesn't. It only takes a few minutes. As soon as we "draw near to Him", He will "draw near to us." It may take a little time to recondition your thought life and daily habits. But just get back to God. How can you tell if you're getting bored? It's when people getting saved, healed, filled with the Spirit, and turned on to God's Word doesn't excite you anymore. The other sign is that bored Preachers also get distracted with loose and false doctrines.

50. **After success of any sort, don't get high and mighty.** Instead, stay humble, stay totally dependent on the Lord through His Spirit, and remain empty of all self-sufficiency. "But when he was strong, [Uzziah's] heart was lifted up" (2 Chronicles 26:16). He became furious with the priests, and leprosy hit him. God knows when our hearts are off, even if what we're doing on the outside is right. "...and [Amaziah] did what was right in the sight of the Lord, but not with a loyal heart" (2 Chronicles 25:2).

51. **Preach as if Jesus walked in.** If He did, how would it change what you say and with what attitude you say it? Are you confident about the revelation you're about to present? Is it clearly respresented in the New Covenant that the Lord Jesus paid His life for? Is there any self exaltation or parading personality that can be detected? Remember, we answer to Him, both now and at the Judgment Seat.

52. **You make the Word of God of no effect by your tradition** (Matthew 15:6). Be careful with church

traditions and cultural traditions that aren't emphasized in New Testament Scripture. Successful church requires that we emphasize important things and de-emphasize lesser things. Ceremonial formalities take up valuable gospel ministry time and put a damper on the spirit, expectancy, and openness of the atmosphere. Things like:

- Endless introductions of people
- Honoring every important person by letting them speak
- Discussing local events or politics
- Singing happy birthday during church meetings is a cultural habit that brings no value to a spiritual setting. A church of 1000 wouldn't sing for everyone's birthday, so why would a church of 50? Find a better time and reason to honor individuals.
- Acknowledging the Jewish calendar and feasts
- Over-doing music or music leaders over-exhorting to the point that people are too worn out to receive much from the teaching or other spiritual ministry
- Wearing priestly apparel—wear what you like, but be careful not to let others put their faith or esteem in clothing, as it's an Old Testament theme that did not pass through the Cross.

Rather, if you want good and healthy church, put all your faith in these scriptural elements:
- Teaching and preaching God's Word with New Testament accuracy and strictness

- The love of God toward one another with healthy fellowship
- Baptism of the Holy Spirit and fire
- Making room for the Holy Spirit to move
- Healing the sick and delivering the oppressed
- Prayer—private and corporate
- Praying in tongues—private and corporate
- Christian purpose—encouraging everyone to both share the Christ with others and also be part of discipling the saints
- Church unity—being in one accord is a prerequisite for spiritual power and glory. When the early Church had one mind, one heart, and one soul, they received great grace from God and demonstrated great power (Acts 2:1, 4:24, 5:12). Remind the saints frequently to abhor strife and to "strive together for the faith of the gospel" (Phillipians 1:27).

Chapter 8
Discipline and Conflict in the Church

There are two types of leaven mentioned in the Bible. One is the leaven of religion, or "works for righteousness", where people try to blend Old Testament law-keeping for righteousness into our New Testament righteousness by faith alone (Galatians 5:9). The other is the leaven of sin and hypocrisy (1 Corinthians 5:6, Luke 12:1). Some have ignored a lot of scriptures to conclude that being under grace means that every church member can do what they want and no one gets to judge them or say anything, but that is completely contrary to the New Testament. So, let's discuss how to deal with sin and conflict in the Church, since those in Ministry Offices and local church governments are ultimately responsible in the sight of God.

1. **Love, mercy, and forgiveness is our guide**, "And above all things have fervent love for one another, for love will cover a multitude of sins" (1 Peter 4:8). No church will succeed without the Pastor and

Ministers understanding the high calling of the love walk. We are not the local church sin police, where every error must be called on the carpet and where everyone's lifestyle is in constant question. Generally, you want to let the ministry of the Word and the Spirit do the convicting for people's lifestyles. Learn to trust God to do the work in people and convince them of needed changes rather than take the burden of it yourself. It's always more successful and powerful when someone hears from the Lord themselves or hears the preaching of the Word to the general assembly and decides on their own, than when they have to be personally reprimanded by a Minister. So, allow most of your rebuking and correcting to come naturally during the teaching and preaching.

2. **Keep the preaching pure**—if you happen to know of people's specific sins or circumstances, do not use that knowledge to target them particularly with your preaching. Do your best to *forget* everyone's details when you preach, so you can keep the ministry pure and so everyone is blessed. There will be many times that people feel you were speaking *just to them* and addressing precisely their own personal circumstance. And it's always a lot better when they know that you didn't know of their circumstance ahead of time. They will receive the preaching much easier. If your motives are pure and you're not using the platform for personal jabs and victories, then knowing when and when not to preach the hard thing will be clear.

3. **Continued, unrepentant sin**—be led by the Spirit as to when and how to address such problems. There

comes a time when those in sin must be confronted. That time is *when others are being affected* by that sin, or when the potential for injury to themselves or others has reached a tipping point. It's one thing when someone is working out their salvation, stumbling, repenting, and getting back up. It's another when they're openly defiant. Basically, our first responsibility is to protect the innocent. Jesus seemed to have great mercy instead of strictness and gave "time to repent"—until someone else was being affected.

> Then He said to the disciples, It is impossible that no offenses should come, but woe to him through whom they do come! It would be better for him if a millstone were hung around his neck, and he were thrown into the sea, than that he should offend one of these little ones (Luke 17:1-2).

At the cross, mercy took the upper hand over punishment. But offending an innocent one and harming other believers is what activates judgment. When Jesus rebuked the church at Thyatira (Revelation 2:18-23) and threatened to destroy Jezebel, it was because she was "teaching My servants to commit fornication". Notice what came first, though, "I gave her space to repent of her fornication, and she did not repent." Forgiveness and mercy is always first, but open, unrepentant sin will spread like leaven if it's not treated.

The fornicator in 1 Corinthians 5 was not judged only because of his fornication, but because others knew about it and knew nothing was being done about it. In a family, the injustice of not disciplining a rebel will cause the others to either lose heart or adopt the same behavior. It is the Pastor who would be responsible to lead the excommunication of a stiff-necked rebellious Christian. In this case, Paul commanded that the man be turned over to "Satan for the destruction of the flesh" with the purpose being, "so that his soul could be saved". This refers to the fact that an unrepentant brother would be put out as open prey for Satan to cause suffering and affliction, and as a result, he would either repent and get back into right church standing, or he would die and go to Heaven before hardening his heart further to the point of disbelief and no return.

> It is actually reported that there is sexual immorality among you, and such sexual immorality as is not even named among the Gentiles—that a man has his father's wife! In the name of our Lord Jesus Christ, when you are gathered together, along with my spirit, with the power of our Lord Jesus Christ, deliver such a one to Satan for the destruction of the flesh, that his spirit may be saved in the day of the Lord Jesus. Your glorying is not good. Do you not know that a little leaven leavens the whole lump? Therefore purge out the old leaven, that you may be a new lump, since you truly are unleavened. For indeed Christ, our Passover, was sacrificed for us... I wrote to you in my epistle not to keep company with sexually immoral people...But now I have written to you not to keep company with anyone named a brother, who is sexually immoral, or covetous, or an idolater, or a

reviler, or a drunkard, or an extortioner, not even to eat with such a person. For what have I to do with judging those also who are outside? Do you not judge those who are inside? But those who are outside God judges. Therefore put away from yourselves the evil person (1 Corinthians 5:1-13).

Notice how we are fully backed and commanded to judge people inside the church for the sake of protecting everyone else. I wouldn't say that turning people over to the devil to speed their repentance should happen very often, but it certainly must be in the realm of possibility because it's a New Testament doctrine. Most churches won't even read this passage, but real Ministers must be prepared for it. Unfortunately, many times, those who've been rebuked will just leave and find another church so they can avoid the repentance, rather than change and come back to the same church.

4. **All correction must be done in the Spirit**, with proper timing, seasoned words, and sincere love, and without anger or frustration,

> But avoid foolish and ignorant disputes, knowing that they generate strife. And a servant of the Lord must not quarrel but be gentle to all, able to teach, patient, in humility correcting those who are in opposition, if God perhaps will grant them repentance, so that they may know the truth (2 Timothy 2:23-25).

5. **Responding to accusations**—the Lord gives us this process:

> ... if your brother sins against you, go and tell him his fault between you and him alone. If he hears you, you have gained your brother. But if he will not hear, take with you one or two more, that 'by the mouth of two or three witnesses every word may be established'. And if he refuses to hear them, tell it to the church. But if he refuses even to hear the church, let him be to you like a heathen and a tax collector (Matthew 18:15-17).

Any accusation against an elder must also be substantiated, "Against an elder receive not an accusation, but before two or three witnesses. Them that sin rebuke before all, that others also may fear" (1 Timothy 5:19-20). Be very careful when accepting an accusation against another Minister, and perform due diligence in getting the facts, as many lives will be affected.

Resolving Conflicts

Because Church involves people, there will always be occasional conflicts. But if we are spiritual and mature, no conflict has to damage the Church or people.

1. **Realize that most divisions occur because two parties never get to the table and lay out all the facts.** Be courageous to do so, for without the facts from both sides, people are left to assumptions and judgments that the devil uses to cause permanent damage to relationships.

2. **Love only focuses on the solution.** There are no impossible people problems if you will think *solutions*—always. Leaders can kill momentum by focusing on the problem rather than the promise, the vision, and the solution. Love doesn't take account of a wrong that is suffered (1 Corinthians 13:5).

3. **The Minister must be the peacemaker.** And the Minister must teach others to be as well. Blessed are the peacemakers. "Peace, if possible—truth at all costs" —Martin Luther.

4. **Ministers absorb everything to protect everyone else**, just like parents do to protect children. Never disclose one person's sin to another, unless it is necessary to train a leader or inform a leader so they can beware of something in order to protect others.

5. **Reactions must always be spiritual.** The relationships and love of God between saints are more important than the outward, immediate task at hand. The Church is a family, and we must stay together. People can't grow and succeed if they're not connected to one another, so work to keep the connection. This means you'll need to restrain yourself when responding to people, "A soft answer turns away wrath, but a harsh word stirs up anger" (Proverbs 15:1).

Chapter 9

Sheep, Goats, Wolves, and Sheepdogs

It is clear that we believers are likened to *sheep* in Scripture, with Jesus being our Great Shepherd and Pastors being His under-shepherds. So, with that analogy, let's add goats, sheepdogs, and wolves into the picture, since sheep and goats are commonly found together in the same fold. It is important for leaders to recognize the differences so that goats are not mistaken for sheep. And wolves must be excommunicated immediately upon being found out. (For this comparison, the goats are not necessarily the ones Jesus is going to separate and cast into the lake of fire. But rather, are believers who are not being very honorable sheep.) [Some premise taken from Mark Barclay's, Sheep, Goats, and Wolves teaching].

Sheep

"For He is our God; and we are the people of His pasture, and the sheep of His hand" (Psalm 95:7).

1. **Sheep are gentle, quiet, innocent, non-aggressive animals**. They do not give their shepherds a lot of

problems. They are very docile animals. They are affectionate and willing to be led.

2. **Sheep are grazers**—unlike goats, which instead like to browse. The sheep enjoy eating in lush green pastures. God's sheep love to eat the Word of God. They love to be in the presence of God. They are hungry and rarely will miss a feeding (a *meeting*). They are not in a hurry to move on and will stay as long as the shepherd allows.

3. **"The Lord is my shepherd**; I shall not want. He makes me to lie down in green pastures: he leads me beside the still waters" (Psalm 23:2). Sheep will lie down and rest in those good fields. Lying down is a sign of passivity and submission. God's sheep would rather submit than fight. Of course, sheep can "baaa" and let their voice be heard, but they don't fight the shepherd. Sheep rarely give the shepherd problems.

4. **Sheep enjoy still waters**, not liking to drink from agitated waters. They love peaceful, quiet conditions. They are not quick to be where strife, arguing, dissension, or turmoil is present. Such problems make the sheep skittish and they are quick to scurry away from such discord.

5. **Sheep like to be sheared**. They don't mind the shepherd taking their wool. And they know they'll grow it back—that shearing is part of the process, and that without it, they will get imbalanced, heavy, and unhealthy. They know they need their shepherd. Sheep don't mind the offering time. They delight in investing their "wool" into the Kingdom more than anywhere else.

6. **Sheep are open to the voice of the Lord**, their Shepherd, "My sheep hear My voice" (John 10:27), whether it's from reading their Bible, listening to the Word preached, or spoken in counsel from a Minister.

Goats

Goats need a shepherd, too. Though they are not as easy to manage as sheep, they are still allowed in the same pasture. They are out of order and must be managed, but they still have much needed "milk" that is useful to the Kingdom and the local church.

1. **Goats are pushy, aggressive, self-sufficient, and headstrong** and can be subtly aggressive in personality to the point of causing undercurrents, dissension, and tension.
2. **Some goats are vocal and obvious. Other goats are silent and fuming.**
3. **Goats like high places** and are always looking for a better position. If you've ever seen a goat in the wild, he's climbing on a rock, or a cliff, or on top of another goat or sheep. They are not herded as well as sheep because they would rather lead than follow. Natural goats walk with their tails held high (possible symbol—pride) and they occasionally emit an unpleasant "air" about them.
4. **Goats want to be recognized** (up high). They secretly want and seek attention and honors—mainly from the Pastor. Advertising one's title is a clear sign of a goat trying to be recognized.

5. **Goats have ulterior motives**, even if it's just a simple self-ambition for validation. Goats are never at rest, always working their agenda. They can't lie down and relax like a sheep.

6. **Goats don't take correction very well.** If rebuked, they just hop the fence. Goats are the ones who pick fights with the Pastor.

7. **If you find yourself "walking on eggshells"** around one of your leaders because they're so easily offended at how you treat or neglect them, they might be goats. You may not even realize it at first because goats can be outwardly quiet and inwardly fuming, but once you notice a bit of difficulty connecting with someone (in the spirit, trying to touch their spirit), be prepared for some goat horns.

8. **Goats are usually "church hoppers".** Goats don't enjoy the green pastures in the same way as the sheep. They are not always satisfied with what the shepherd (leader) gives them. Like a goat in the wild, they nibble here and there, sampling a variety of bushes and leaves. Because they are browsers and do not graze, they tend to wander when they eat. Goats will always have a substantial history of churches on their "resume", as longevity is not their strong suit. (*Church hopping is for babies, just as fornication is for unfaithful teenagers. Marriage and covenant-making is for adults and mature people. Once you commit to one, you leave the others alone, even if there are challenges. Enjoy yours, and stop looking over the fence.*)

9. **Goats aren't all bad all the time.** First of all, they can be milked, which is a blessing to others. Also, they will not eat the sheep because they are not the meat

eaters that the wolves are. They may be agitators and cause some turmoil for the shepherd, but they are not seriously harmful to the sheep. Perhaps that is why Jesus waits until His return to separate the sheep from the goats. But there's something about a hard headed goat. At midnight, when the moon is full and their heart reaches the tipping point of bitterness and envy, somehow they turn into wolves! At that point, they have no problem hurting a few sheep during their exit.

10. **With a little repentance and humility, goats can become sheep.**

Wolves

1. **"Beware of false prophets, who come to you in sheep's clothing**, but inwardly they are ravenous wolves" (Matthew 7:15). Wolves look like sheep. They sometimes look like leaders. But they are dangerous to be around. They are hungry and selfish and don't care who they hurt. Have mercy on people who are honest, sincere, and teachable, but have no mercy on demons. Demons will attack ministries, so get those people out who are being used by the devil or who are prideful and won't receive instruction.

2. **"Go your way; behold, I send you out as lambs among wolves"** (Luke 10:3). You can't kill the wolves. You just have to be aware of them and keep people safe from them. And at some point, once the wolf is found out, he's kicked out of the pasture.

3. **Wolves won't be found near the Pastor very often.** They will stay away from him because they know

they're in error. Rather, they will search out the weaker sheep. They are sly, and when any issue or dissention arises, they will pounce on it and use it for their advantage—to capture a sheep (gain some favor somehow).

4. **When the Pastor is absent**, wolves (and sometimes goats), see that as their opportunity to advance their agenda. "After my departure savage wolves will come in, not sparing the flock" (Acts 20:29). This could be when a Pastor goes out of town, when a Pastor dies, or simply when not present at a meeting. The issue is that wolves don't really care about the flock or the individual sheep, and therefore they prey on the ones who are weak.

5. **Wolves are very deceptive.** Wolves wear sheep's clothing and will trick many people who are not spiritually trained. When you perceive something in the spirit, take note of it. If it doesn't change, seek the Lord on when and how to address it before the wolf sheds its costume. What are the signs? Wolves may sound sweet, but the way they handle people is rough. Know them by their fruits (Matthew 7:16)—are they interested in people, or do they not bother after they've "done their thing"? Do they promote an atmosphere of peace and unity, or of discord?

6. **Wolves are sheep stealers.** And they don't care how it affects people ("not sparing the flock"). When people are persuaded to leave a church for no apparent reason, it always causes confusion. The other sheep are left with thoughts of: *Did they get*

eaten by the wolf? Did the shepherd crucify them and have them for supper? Can I feel safe still in this pasture?

7. **A good shepherd gives his life for the sheep**, just like Jesus. A hireling is an uncommitted leader and a "thief and a robber", who doesn't really care about the Church or the people.

   > I am the good shepherd. The good shepherd gives His life for the sheep. But a hireling, he who is not the shepherd, one who does not own the sheep, sees the wolf coming and leaves the sheep and flees; and the wolf catches the sheep and scatters them. The hireling flees because he is a hireling and does not care about the sheep (John 10:11-13).

8. **King David's son Absalom was a wolf**. After much friction in his life and with his father, Absalom began calling men to himself. He would sit at the gate of the city and kiss everyone's hand who came through, offering to be their judge and settle all their disputes "justly", making them all feel real good, "So Absalom stole the hearts of the men of Israel" (2 Samuel 15:6). This happens in churches, where one leader very deceptively, with a smiling face, steals the hearts of the people. They casually drop doubtful statements about the Pastor or other leaders. Before you know it, they've dragged all sorts of unsuspecting people out the door with them and pulled them all out of the will of God. Absalom caused a lot of innocent deaths in his rebellion, including his own. Wolves are so selfish that they don't care. True shepherds put their sheep first and

do whatever is necessary to hold God's people together.

Sheepdogs

Sheepdogs are also found in a pasture, with a shepherd, and near the flocks of sheep and goats. There's no Scriptural reference, but we can sure find a place for them in a church analogy.

1. **Sheepdogs aide the shepherds in keeping the sheep safe**, keeping the goats corralled, and keeping the wolves out. Sheepdogs are leaders who help the Pastor by keeping an eye and an ear out, nipping the heels of sheep that are straying, barking occasionally if a goat is out of line, and fighting wolves if necessary.

2. **Sheepdogs are well trained to protect the flock.** They form the perimeter. They gain the respect of the wolves, who know to stay away.

3. **Sheepdogs don't turn on the shepherd.** They are not there to protect the sheep *from the shepherd*, but the sheep *from the wolves* and the devil. Never will you pass by a field and see a sheepdog nipping at the heels of a shepherd chasing him around and around. Rather, they *help* the shepherd. Pastor Mark Barclay says that if the watchdogs pal around with the wolves and get a taste for lamb chops, they might one day turn into a wolf. But good watchdogs won't.

4. **Sheepdogs may bark** to let their voice be heard by the shepherd, but they won't bite him or leave him unless he is unruly.

Chapter 10
Ministry Etiquette for Pastors and Traveling Ministers

Pastors don't always understand traveling Ministers. Traveling Ministers don't always understand Pastors. It's important to "step into each other's shoes" for a moment in order to foster a good working relationship with the benefit of the Church in mind.

Etiquette for Pastors

1. **Realize that you are responsible to get other preaching Gifts before the people.** Some Pastors don't want anyone else ministering to their people. That's not Scriptural nor healthy. And don't choose only those who minister to your own preferences and at your own level, but realize how your members will benefit from various Ministers. Without input from other Ministry Gifts, your congregation's needs will not be met.

2. **Partnering**—find traveling Preachers and missionaries that you can share some of your church

tithes and offerings with every month. It's good for both your church and them. Since most Kingdom finances flow through the local church, Pastors have a huge responsibility to consider the traveling Preachers. Certainly, it must be done without pressure. And certainly, traveling Preachers must be adding consistent value to the Church at large and not just sitting around at home or taking vacations. But every church should have a few Preacher partners (and not just the ones on television). So, use your faith and connect with someone outside your church.

3. **Treat traveling Ministers with honor and respect.** Make them feel welcome when they preach for you. Consider their preferences, preparation time, and rest needs. When you pick them up for ministry, try not to run personal errands, make small talk, or force them into sightseeing or leisure activities.

4. **Care for their traveling needs as best you can.** Use your faith. Find out their preferences for the time before meetings (eating, fellowship, etc.) and be cognizant of their demeanor. Communicate up front what's expected and what you will do. And do what you say. Pay for their travel expenses when possible.

5. **Give them adequate leeway in the service.** Keep the music time and preliminaries shorter, rather than indulge all of your normal church activities. Allow your people to fully open the gift of God in the guest Preacher, since he or she is only present for a short time. Consider multiple meetings for that purpose.

6. **Wisdom about anointing**—recognize that the spirit and anointing the guest Preacher carries can cause the atmosphere to be heightened, but that doesn't mean the Pastor or worship leader should indulge themselves in preaching or ministering. Let the guest Preacher who brought the particular anointing initiate things. The Pastor should keep the overall authority, but give the guest Preacher pre-eminence in most cases. For example, when an Evangelist is present, it's not appropriate to take fifteen minutes telling your evangelism stories before you welcome the person to the microphone. If a Prophet has come, it's not appropriate to let the spirit of the Prophet get on you and use it to preach or prophesy.

7. **Make it a practice to always receive a love offering *after*** the guest Preacher has ministered and not before (or if necessary, near the end before an altar call or ministry time). This allows the people to return material things for the spiritual things they have received. Occasionally it makes sense to give an honorarium (a determined amount) instead of receiving an offering; but if you do, be sure it is an adequate one and not too far from what they might have received if the people were involved. Whatever you do, never muzzle the ox that treads the corn.

   No skimming off the guest Minister's offering. And keep a guest Minister's offering separate from your meeting expenses, using your faith to pay for their expenses out of your own budget if possible, giving the *entire* offering to the traveling Minister. If you're not able to do that, collect an expense offering in a separate and distinct manner, and communicate it clearly to the traveling Minister.

8. **Protect the guest Minister from being "mauled" by church members** before and after the service, who may tend to take up too much time telling life stories or wanting personal ministry.

9. **Be sensitive to the scale of ministry you are bringing in.** For traveling Ministers with an exceptional grace upon them for ministering to large crowds and having a full schedule, it doesn't make sense to ask them to come preach at a small, startup church. Their weeks are numbered just like everyone else's, and even though pure Ministers are not in it for the money, their monthly budget is very steep to pay employees and expenses. And money aside—their impact at large is greater when ministering to hundreds rather than tens, so think of the whole rather than only the part. Of course, the Holy Spirit may set it up and put it on both Ministers' hearts, and that would be fine. Just be wise, and use your faith to allow God to provide for the guest Preacher above and beyond what may be normal compensation from your church.

10. **Be respectful to traveling Ministers who contact you** looking for a connection or place to preach. Trust that their motive is right and that they are doing what they believe is of the Lord, trying to get their Gift out. So consider their appeal, take a glimpse at their ministry materials, and give them an honest answer as you prayerfully consider, accept, or decline their offer.

Etiquette for Traveling Ministers

1. **Honor the local church authority**. Even if you may feel "over" the Pastor *in the Lord*, you are not over him in the *local church setting*. The Pastor is the highest authority in the local church, so strengthen him and substantiate him in the eyes of the people. Never rebuke the Pastor or correct a church activity in front of the people. Speak to the Pastor in private only if the Lord directs you.

   Never belittle the Pastor, even in jest. For example, if you use an illustration where you pull volunteers up on the stage, never choose the Pastor (not even if it's for the role of Pastor). Pastors have enough trouble with lack of esteem in the church without your adding to it. Choose someone else for your props rather than make the Pastor stand up there looking uncomfortable.

2. **Remember that you are building on another man's foundation**. Even if that foundation is a bit shaky, it's what they are living on, so tread lightly. It's funny to say, "Well, I'm the Evangelist, so I blow in, blow up, and blow out." But don't actually do that. Remember the wake that you leave will be cleaned up by the Pastor, so don't make it difficult on him. Don't open up controversial topics, preach your pet doctrines, or go out "on a limb" with some new teaching without first speaking to the Pastor about it. Pastors don't need you to bring a fancy new

message or revelation, but rather to impart something of yourself from your own special grace that edifies the people. Pastors don't need to be pointed or directed with new vision. Let God do that.

3. **"Always bless the local church, and you'll always have a place to preach"**—Kenneth Hagin. If you are there to promote your ministry, or if you preach flimsy doctrine, you are not blessing that church. Be there to assist the Pastor in building up the people and growing the church. Seek the Lord to bring the right message.

4. **Don't bring some eccentric list of personal preference demands with you.** No matter how grand your ministry becomes, be a good "missionary", and don't be a high-minded prima donna. Sleep where they put you. Ride in what they provide. And eat and drink what is offered to you. And if asked for your preference on food or amenities, be reasonable and considerate in your requests and travel costs.

5. **Listen and communicate well concerning the Pastor's ministry expectations**, time restraints, expense details, etc. And adhere to them.

6. **Believe God for open doors before seeking them** (Rev 3:7, Acts 10:34, Col 4:3-4, 2 Cor 2:12, 1 Cor 16:9, Prov 18:16, Matt 7:7-8, John 14:13-14). Be led by the Spirit and trust God to direct your steps. It's okay to contact Pastors, but don't be pushy. Just present yourself as you're led by the Spirit, and leave it at that. Look to build relationships with Pastors more than just acquire a place to preach. Remind

Pastors what you do and give media samples of your ministry when appropriate. Pastors have a lot going on already, so they need time to consider your offer or to put it "on the shelf" for a while. And you may certainly need to plant another seed many months later.

7. **Trust God to give you partners in ministry rather than be aggressive or manipulative.** Keep a right motive for your mailing list or your contacting people. Isn't it only to minister the Word to them? If you do things right, God will always provide.

8. **Trust God for your offering amounts rather than make demands on a church.** Sometimes, God will want you to preach where you spend more money than you receive. So do it cheerfully, and let God make up the difference later.

9. **For overseas ministries**, it is *not* okay to solicit churches around the world to support your work. Formal emails and letters of how you want to join a ministry, without having read their books, watched their videos, or learned from that ministry, carries a wrong, money-seeking motive with it. If you don't need teaching and ministry from other ministries, then you must obviously be mature enough to know God as your Source and not need money from them either. Ask God to connect you properly, and be honest in your dealings.

10. **Your ministry is probably not going to be that of "encouraging Pastors"**, especially if you're just starting out. For some reason, we've seen the occasional new Preacher decide that God wanted him going around to preach to Pastors. It doesn't

work that way. To encourage Pastors, you will need deep friendship with Pastors, or you will need to have *raised up* Pastors, or you will need enough seasoned ministry experience so that they are coming to *you*.

11. **Be at your best and give your best every time.** Don't be lazy or bored with your primary gift / anointing and start dabbling in some other thing that's not as effective and not the will of God.

Chapter 11
Solid Doctrine

1. **The winds of doctrine are always blowing.** But they won't affect you if you're rock solid in your Bible knowledge.

2. **It's not always completely false doctrine that messes people up, but *winds* of doctrine** that blow Ministers and churches around, "...carried about by every wind of doctrine..." (Ephesians 4:14). Sometimes, what people do and preach is *completely* wrong and offensive, but other times it is more like substituting *brass* for *gold*. Brass may not kill you, but don't we want God's best? We want the gold. Baby Christians are sometimes very satisfied with brass *everything*. But Ministers ought to know the difference and not get babies addicted to something less than pure gold.

3. **Recognizing error**—to do this consistently, it requires sincere commitment to God's Word and honest spiritual evaluation of our doctrines and emphasis. Not everything done in the Name of Jesus is spiritual, and some of it is even dangerous to people's faith. Having good discernment does not mean that you are critical or judgmental, but it also doesn't mean you should be silent. We have a Scriptural obligation to point out wrong doctrine, but usually it's best to leave out people's names

unless someone has blatantly and publicly gone twisted.

4. **Just because something is popular with television ministries or big churches doesn't mean it's right.** There's a lot of peer pressure in some ministry circles. But if it's not perfectly Scriptural, and if it's not your personal mandate from the Lord, don't fall for it.

5. **Don't feed their itching ears.** Don't try to seek out new revelation that goes beyond stable Bible doctrine. Don't look to tickle people's ears to attract them to your ministry. Emphasize the simple and complete New Testament gospel of the Lord Jesus Christ, "For the time will come when they will not endure sound doctrine, but according to their own desires, because they have itching ears, they will heap up for themselves teachers" (2 Timothy 4:3).

Areas of Doctrinal Conflict

Here are some areas of conflict that you will certainly encounter as a Minister, and you will need clear Scriptural precision to prove them out, establish your position in the Lord about them, and answer people. This is only a mention of a few topics and not necessarily an exhaustive list.

Some topics have suggested reference books. And you can find teachings for others on our Ministers School web page: http://stevensonministries.org/ministers

1. **Cessasionists**—those who hold the unscriptural view that supernatural tongues and miracles have ceased. You will need to be able to prove out the truth.

2. **Baptize in the Name of Jesus only**—there is still one or two Christian denominations that are hung up on the words spoken over a person when they are dunked in water, saying that a person isn't really saved if the proper sentence is not said, when truly it only matters that the person has faith in Christ.

3. **Theodicy, suffering, sovereignty**—theodicy is the practice of trying to logically vindicate God's goodness and justice in the face of the existence of suffering and evil. It is basically the *sovereignty* belief system vs. the *faith and human responsibility* belief system. The problem occurs when people try to explain God and evil through the exercise of reason and logic alone *without right scriptural logic.* (Refer to the book, *God, Why?*—by Chas Stevenson.)

4. **Righteousness, grace, forgiveness of sins**—for a powerful clarification of and solution to the grace controversy, refer to the book, *The Real Grace*—by Chas Stevenson.

5. **Faith and healing**—be prepared to explain the prayer of faith and God's healing covenant, and answer the tough questions like *why do some people not get healed?, what about Paul's thorn?, what about Job?*, and more. And learn to get people healed!

6. **The unpardonable sin**—the one unforgivable sin is definite and permanent rejection of Christ (John 3:18, 3:36). Blasphemy of the Holy Spirit is when the Spirit has revealed Christ to a person's heart and

they reject Christ from their heart. If a person is concerned that they may have committed the unpardonable sin, they haven't. The concern about it is evidence that they haven't.

7. **Universalism**—some have twisted Scripture to imply that since Jesus died on the cross to save the entire world, that everyone is automatically saved. Clearly, John 3:36 and 1 John 5:12 refute that.

8. **Women Preachers**—the scriptures that have been used to silence women in churches have nothing to do with a mandate from God about who is called into pulpit ministry. Rather, those scriptures are in the context of keeping order in the marriage relationship—that the wife should not usurp authority over her husband and over-speak him (1 Corinthians 14:34-36, 1 Timothy 2:11-12). The Greek word for *women* is 'gune', but so is the Greek word for *wives*. So, if you study those scriptures in that light, it has nothing to do with women and wives not talking at church or having leadership roles, but rather wives keeping their submission to their husbands apparent in public.

9. **Overdoing music**—be careful of the unscriptural emphasis being placed on music time in the Church. Because the New Testament is silent on the issue, we should not be making it a paramount doctrine. Music is a *help*, but not an end unto itself. What has happened around the world is that people are more excited about the music time than they are about the ministry of the Word and Spirit. It takes faith and emphasis to correct this and mature a congregation.

10. **The false church**—beware of the modern day *false church* trend. What is that? It's the contemporary trend these days to compromise certain beliefs and practices from the Word of God in order to "not offend people" so they will stay in the church. Staying relevant is great. But compromising the Word or true Spirit-filled gospel ministry is wrong.

11. **The Israel affair**—neither Jesus nor any Apostle ever commanded the Church to do anything with natural Israel or unbelieving Jews except preach the gospel to them and try to turn them to Christ. Emphasizing Old Testament practices, Jewish traditions, or natural Jerusalem herself is not part of our current, New Testament gospel work of turning people from darkness to light and from the power of satan to God (Acts 26:18). Any attention given to natural Israel must be kept in perspective as a personal interest and not as a Christian command or pursuit.

12. **LGBT and homosexuality** (Lesbian, Gay, Bisexual, Transgendered)—the homosexuality and sexual perversion issue is not going away. The "god of tolerance" is the new god for unsaved society today. So, Ministers must be prepared to answer the topic with grace, seasoned with salt, with compassion for those needing help and with wisdom for those looking for a fight.

13. **Alcohol and drugs**—a Minister must be "not given to wine" (1 Timothy 3:3). "It is not for kings to drink wine; nor for princes strong drink: lest they drink and forget the [Word]" (Proverbs 31:4-5), and all Christians are *kings and priests unto God* (Revelation 1:6). "Wine is a mocker, strong drink is raging: and

whosoever is deceived thereby is not wise" (Proverbs 20:1). Drunkenness is a sin. And so is "tipsy". Being a stumbling block to others is a sin. Alcohol has bad spiritual consequences, "Whoredom and wine and new wine take away the heart", or "Liquor and lust deprive them of their wits" (Hosea 4:11, Moffat's).

14. **Demonology**—Ministers must be prepared to cast devils out using the Name of Jesus and the power of the Holy Spirit. But stay Scriptural, and don't overemphasize evil spirits and deliverance. Also know that sitting under the Word of God and humbly responding in faith to it can cause great deliverance, and it is required for lasting deliverance. (Refer to *The Triumphant Church*—by Kenneth E. Hagin.)

15. **Generational curses**—certainly, there are sins and afflictions that permeate and continue in a family through the years. In the Old Testament, disobedience could sometimes warrant the curse carrying down through three or four generations. In the New Testament, however, we recognize that everyone is affected by the curse to some degree, and that now, "Christ has redeemed us from the curse" (Galatians 3:13). At salvation, we can all access deliverance from all the curse, all the sickness, and all the demonic oppression our family has dealt with. We only need faith in the work of the cross, the Name of Jesus, and in the power of God. It doesn't have to be an ominous process, but rather an exercise of determined authority.

16. **Hyper spirituality**—being spiritual does not mean a person is always seeing things in the spirit realm,

never knowing what to really do with them or what they mean. Rather, being spiritual means that we are secure in our heart, mature in the love of God, and effective in recognizing and helping others. Sometimes, a strong desire for personal spiritual manifestations will open the door to familiar spirits. How can you tell? If the so called "spiritual person" is frequently oppressed rather than free and rejoicing, and if the things they are seeing never really help anyone, it is probably not of God.

17. **Prophetic superstition, dreams, and visions**—astronomy and lunar eclipses predict nothing for the Church of Jesus Christ, but are only a flimsy, superstitious attempt to find spiritual meaning in something natural. The "lights in the ... heavens" were not for prophetic signs, but for natural, nautical, directional signs. God never used stars and moons for divine events and never told us to. Dreams and visions can occasionally be of God, but if so, they will not be confusing, "God is not the author of confusion" (1 Corinthians 14:33). They will have a clear message attached to the image seen, as the message is the main thing and the image is only a stamp to solidify its permanence in our minds. Also, if a dream or vision is from God, there will be no fear attached. Something from God will be clear and edifying rather than ominous and threatening. There is no such thing as a "dream interpretation ministry", where every color, number, and scenario provides the formula for a spiritual message. Even numerology ministry causes misplaced faith, as it's a flimsy attempt at revelation knowledge. Certainly, it seems there are some

number patterns that God used before the cross of Christ. But never did Jesus, Paul, Peter, John, James, nor Jude instruct the Church to follow numbers, use numbers, or get prophetic meaning from numbers today. Born again, new covenant, Spirit filled people have no need for tying numbers into life's coincidences.

18. **The second coming of Jesus Christ**—remember to teach the end times to new Christians, for it is a foundational doctrine that establishes a definite hope for the future (Hebrews 6—resurrection of the dead and eternal judgment—Christians answer for and are rewarded for the things done in the body, but there is no "whipping post" for believers). Once you decide for yourself when the catching away of the saints occurs (pre-tribulation, post-tribulation, or mid-tribulation), be sure to include "most likely" and "possibly" somewhere in your teaching. Scriptures seem to lean toward a definite pre-tribulation rapture, but there are also a few questions that arise. Whichever you subscribe to, the one thing that is clear is that true believers will be exempted from the doom of the world one way or the other, as God has never punished the righteous along with the unrighteous. And don't ever try and pick the date for His return. Somehow, even good Preachers, who sometimes seem to get bored in their later years, decide to wow the Church with their predictions. Don't do it. Not even Jesus knows that day and hour, so why try to know more than Him? (Mark 13:32).

Other Theological Terms and Concepts

This handbook is prepared with the expectation that the Minister has already become adept at the Word of God by either personal or formal study. However, the list below is to fill any gaps so that the Minister is not caught off guard by terminology, and also for the Minister to round out his or her training with further study of church history and impartation from some of our pioneers of faith.

Theology
Theocracy
Spiritology
Soteriology
Ecclesiology
Eschatology
Calvinism vs. Arminianism
Glossalalia
Covenants Old = First (Abrahamic—circumcision of the flesh), New = Second (In Christ—the circumcision of the heart).
Incarnation
Exegesis vs. Isogesis
Hermeneutics
Apologetics

Homiletics
Torah
Pentateuch
Talmud
Septuagint
Providence
Canonical
Dispensationalism
Epistles
Eucharist
Humanism (secular)
Dogma
Gnostics
Agnostics
CE and BCE (AD and BC)

Church Revival History: Protestant Reformation, 1st Great Awakening, 2nd Great Awakening, 3rd Great Awakening, Welsh Revival, Asuza Street & Pentecostal Outpouring, Healing Revival (1948-1957), Charismatic Renewal, Faith and Teaching Revival

Pioneers of Faith: Martin Luther, John Wesley, George Whitfield, Charles Finney, John Knox, D.L. Moody, John Hyde, Billy Sunday, Charles Spurgeon, John Dowie, William Seymour, Charles Parham, John G. Lake, Smith Wigglesworth, Maria Woodworth Etter, Amiee Simple McPherson, F.F. Bosworth, Billy Graham, William Brahnam, Raymond T. Richey, A.A. Allen, T.L. Osborn, Oral Roberts, Lester Sumrall, Kenneth E. Hagin, and many more...

Suggested Resources

The Dake Annotated Reference Bible is a must have study tool for every Minister. In scope and accuracy, it is the most comprehensive and precise there is. And though not perfect in all opinions (no commentary is), you'll find the reference connections and thoroughness supernatural and inspiring.

Finis Jennings Dake was an American Minister in the twentieth century who spent forty years and about 100,000 hours in his lifetime preparing this exposition of God's Word. It is known of Dake that immediately upon his conversion at age seventeen, he was able to quote hundreds of scriptures he had never memorized. As it turned out, he subsequently and without mental memorization was able to quote the entire New Testament, word for word, with chapter and verse, and with punctuation, without looking at any page. A radio station heard of this and contacted Dake, who agreed to demonstrate it if they would put him on the air. They did and he did. It was a gift from God that he dedicated himself to in order to contribute his annotated Bible to the Church before his death.

Other resource recommendations are available upon request. For a full list, contact Stevenson Ministries.

The Fellowship
Of the Unashamed

I am a part of the fellowship of the Unashamed. I have the Holy Spirit Power. The die has been cast. I have stepped over the line. The decision has been made. I am a disciple of Jesus Christ. I won't look back, let up, slow down, back away, or be still. My past is redeemed, my present makes sense, and my future is secure. I am finished and done with low living, sight walking, small planning, smooth knees, colorless dreams, tame visions, mundane talking, chintzy giving, and dwarfed goals.

I no longer need preeminence, prosperity, position, promotions, plaudits, or popularity. I don't have to be right, first, tops, recognized, praised, regarded, or rewarded. I now live by presence, learn by faith, love by patience, lift by prayer, and labor by power.

My pace is set, my gait is fast, my goal is Heaven, my road is narrow, my way is rough, my companions few, my Guide is reliable, my mission is clear. I cannot be bought, compromised, deterred, lured away, turned back, diluted, or delayed. I will not flinch in the face of sacrifice, hesitate in the presence of adversity, negotiate at the table of the enemy, ponder at the pool of popularity, or meander in the maze of mediocrity.

I won't give up, back up, let up, or shut up until I've preached up, prayed up, paid up, stored up, and stayed up for the cause of Christ. I am a disciple of Jesus Christ. I must go until He returns, give until I drop, preach until all know, and work until He comes.

And when He comes to get His own, He will have no problem recognizing me. My colors will be clear for "I am not ashamed of the Gospel, because it is the power of God for the salvation of everyone who believes."

—Dr. Bob Moorehead

Bibliography

Dake, Finis Jennings, *Dake Annotated Reference Bible*, 1963, Dake Publishing, p. 185

Finney, Charles, *Lectures on Revivals of Religion*, 1835, Leavitt, Lord & Co., p. 214,228

Jones, Doug, *Mastering the Silence*, 2004, Kenneth Hagin Ministries, p. 1

Kenyon, E.W., *Two Kinds of Righteousness*, 1989, Kenyons Gospel Publisher, p. 14

Lake, John G., *John G. Lake* 1994, Kenneth Copeland Publications, p. 101, 105

Lane, Bo, "Why Do So Many Pastors Leave the Ministry? The Facts Will Shock You." *EXPASTORS*, January 27, 2014, http://www.expastors.com/why-do-so-many-pastors-leave-the-ministry-the-facts-will-shock-you/

Sherman, Daniel, "Pastor Burnout Statistics." *Pastor Burnout*, 2014, http://www.pastorburnout.com/pastor-burnout-statistics.html

About the Authors

Chas and Joni Stevenson are the founders of *Stevenson Ministries* and also the founders and Pastors of *Houston Faith Church*, an exciting and growing church in Houston, Texas.

Chas' ministry to the Church at large is marked with a refreshing demonstration of God's Word and power that quiets the emotions, stirs the spirit, and brings people back to their high calling of God in Christ. With New Testament devotion to precise, scriptural logic, Chas is a foundation builder of God's Word in people, holding nothing back in igniting people's faith toward God while keeping them committed to the integrity of God's Word.

Joni's ministry is as a Prophet with a piercing preaching gift that revives and edifies the Church with a grace that elevates people into the glory of God and ignites their faith and passion for Christ. Joni ministers with powerful healings and miracles as she flows with the Holy Spirit to demonstrate the power of God and confirm the *right on* message she brings.

FOR MORE FAITH RESOURCES & INFORMATION...
CONNECT WITH US!

Stevenson ministries

www.StevensonMinistries.org

DOWNLOAD OUR PHONE APP

HFC App
(HOUSTON FAITH CHURCH)

ONLINE COURSES with CHAS STEVENSON

A FAITH WALK with Chas & Joni

www.ingramcontent.com/pod-product-compliance
Lightning Source LLC
Chambersburg PA
CBHW071849090426
42811CB00004B/533